Introduction

Measures of trend inflation play an important role in the study of inflation in many countries. In the context of policy analysis, the level and variability of trend inflation can be viewed as barometers of the degree to which inflation expectations in a particular country remain anchored over time. In addition, an estimate of trend inflation can serve as a useful centering point in the construction of inflation forecasts at different horizons. The existing literature has also found that a substantial amount of the observed persistence of international inflation data are accounted for by variations in trend inflation, often related to changes in monetary regimes; see, for example, Levin and Piger (2004), Cecchetti, Hooper, Kasman, Schoenholtz, and Stock and Watson (2007), and Wright (2011).[1]

In this paper, we present estimates of the level and time-varying uncertainty of trend inflation for fourteen advanced economies. The estimates are derived from a multivariate model that pools information from different inflation series for each country. The model is applied on a country-by-country basis, in contrast to an approach of pooling information across countries (such as in Ciccarelli and Mojon, 2010). Our motivation for this choice is twofold: First, the country-by-country approach allows comparing different trend models across different samples of data. Second, while there are clearly some cross-country comovements in overall inflation, such common factors do not necessarily correspond to the components of a trend-cycle decomposition, as confirmed for example by Ciccarelli and Mojon (2010). In particular, as will be shown below, there are also considerable differences in each country's trend estimates, reflecting country-specific developments in monetary regimes and other forces.

Formally, we adopt the definition of trend inflation as the infinite horizon forecast of inflation. This trend definition corresponds to the Beveridge-Nelson (1981) concept, which has been applied to inflation data in a number of studies, including Stock and Watson (2007, 2010), Cecchetti et al. (2007), Clark and Doh (2011) and Cogley, Sargent, and Surico (2013), with variants of the approach also employed by Cogley and Sargent (2005), Cogley, Primiceri, and Sargent (2010) and Kozicki and Tinsley (2012).[2] Our multivariate model builds in the

---

[1] See also Cogley and Sbordone (2009) and Ireland (2007) for the United States specifically.
[2] Cogley and Sargent (2005) and Cogley, Primiceri, and Sargent (2010) derive their measure of trend inflation from a non-linear function of time-varying VAR coefficients is identical to the Beveridge-Nelson trend in approximation.

assumption that, for a given country, different inflation measures share the same common trend. Specifically, we consider percentage changes in core and headline CPI as well as percentage changes in the GDP deflator, proceeding on the assumption that the deviations that these inflation series exhibit from the common trend are stationary.

Our multivariate model nests the popular unobserved components model with stochastic volatility, simply known as "UCSV" model, of Stock and Watson (2007, 2010) that has been applied to inflation data for the G7 countries by Cecchetti, Hooper, Kasman, Schoenholtz, and Watson (2007). The multivariate extension of the UCSV model and the comparison between both models across different countries is the specific contribution of this paper.

The multivariate model presented here extends the UCSV approach in two dimensions. First, as in Mertens (2011), the model extracts its trend estimates from multiple inflation series, instead of conditioning on a single inflation measure. Second, while deviations from trend are assumed to be serially uncorrelated in the UCSV model, inflation gaps can be, and typically are, persistent in our model, but are constrained to be stationary, which proves to have a considerable effect on trend estimates.

As in the UCSV model, we keep track of two measures of stochastic volatility: one for trend shocks and the second one capturing changes in gap volatility. What makes the model tractable is the assumption that a single stochastic volatility measure drives changes in the volatility of all three gaps in our model.[3] A more general approach, embedding separate stochastic volatilities for each gap, would not only be more costly to compute but even much less sensible to implement in our data sample, when there is missing data.[4] In the same vein, we have also chosen to limit time-variation in model parameters to stochastic volatility, keeping inflation gap persistence constant.[5] Our model is thus capable of capturing time-variation in the importance of

---

Kozicki and Tinsley's (2012) refer to their measure as the "shifting endpoint of inflation expectations." In a similar spirit, Levin and Piger (2004) relate time-variation in inflation persistence to structural breaks in the intercepts of autoregressive time-series models for inflation.

[3] Gap shocks can have arbitrary correlations as well as relative variances, for tractability these statistics are however assumed to be time-invariant in our model.

[4] Our approach of restricting stochastic volatility to a scale factor operating on multiple variables follows Carriero, Clark, and Marcellino (2012), who report considerable improvements in fit and accuracy, compared to an unrestricted approach, in Bayesian VARs.

[5] For the United States, see the Cogley and Sargent (2005) and Cogley, Primiceri, and Sargent (2010) studies noted above.

permanent and transitory components of inflation, while abstracting from time-variation in the autocorrelation of the inflation gap process.

In the spirit of the UCSV model, our model yields an autoregressive representation for the inflation process, while remaining silent about potential linkages between inflation and other economic variables, such as measures of capital utilization or the output gap. This is not to say that such linkages might be unimportant or uninteresting to study. But since trend estimates hinge on a model's forecasting properties, and since the marginal importance of other economic variables for forecasting inflation has been shown to be modest at best—as summarized, for example, by Stock and Watson (2009) and Faust and Wright (2012)—attention is limited here on autoregressive models of the inflation process.

Since our estimation relies on state-space methods, with a limited number of time-varying parameters, we can well handle cases in which observations are missing for particular inflation series. Throughout, our estimation uses data since 1960; consequently, for some countries, missing data occur because of limited data availability. Furthermore, we also consider estimates that are conditioned on datasets for which observations on inflation have been discarded for certain dates, because of concern that the available data reflects price shifts due to non-market factors—like outright price controls or tax changes. In doing so, we expand on a number of earlier studies including Gordon (1983), Levin and Piger (2004), and Neiss and Nelson (2005), to name but a few. The inclusion of such price shift dates seems to have some effect on trend estimates, in particular in the case of the UCSV model, whereas our multivariate estimates appear robust to the inclusion of such periods in the estimation.

Finally, we compare the forecast performance of our multivariate model against the UCSV model and the random walk forecasts of Atkeson and Ohanian (2001) in a (pseudo-)real-time evaluation of inflation forecasts from 1985 through 2012. Across forecast horizons ranging from one-quarter to 4-years ahead, our multivariate extension consistently reduced the root mean squared errors ("RMSE") for predictions in most countries, at times by 20 percent or more. But in only a few cases, notably medium-term forecasts for the United States, the improvements are statistically significant.

The remainder of this paper is structured as follows: Section 2 describes our dataset for 14 industrialized countries. Section 3 lays out the empirical models used throughout the paper. Section 4 presents estimates for level and variability of trend inflation derived from univariate and multivariate models. Section 5 reviews periods in which price shifts occurred and their influence on the estimates. Section 6 evaluates (pseudo-)real-time estimates of trend inflation derived from the UCSV model and our preferred conditioned on (pseudo-)real-time data and Section 7 analyzes the forecast performance of our model in real time. Section 8 concludes the paper.

2. International Inflation Data

Our dataset consists of quarterly inflation data for 14 developed countries from 1960:Q1 through 2012:Q4. To the extent that data availability permits, we use three different inflation measures for each country: headline CPI, core CPI and the GDP deflator, all computed as annualized quarterly log-differences. Details on the available data for each country are provided in Table 1. All CPI data are obtained from the *Main Economic Indicators* database produced by the OECD.[6] All GDP deflator data are obtained from the *International Financial Statistics* electronic database maintained by the IMF with the exception of the deflator series for Sweden; the latter series is from the *Main Economic Indicators*.[7] All GDP deflator series from the *IFS* are seasonally adjusted except for Belgium, Ireland and Sweden.

Following Faust and Wright (2012), we apply the X-12-ARIMA filter maintained by the U.S. Census Bureau to each inflation series analyzed in this paper.[8] As the GDP deflator data displayed strong seasonal components—despite being labeled "seasonally adjusted"[9]—we ran the filter over these series as a precaution.

[Table 1 about here]

---

[6] The only exception is the data for Ireland's headline CPI, which was compiled from the *IMF's International Financial Statistics*.
[7] The two exceptions are the GDP deflators for Italy and Japan. The data provided in *IFS* exhibited rebasing problems, so deflator series from Stock and Watson (2003) starting in 1960:Q1 were spliced together with *IFS* data from 2000:Q1 to 2012:Q4.
[8] Complete documentation on the X-12-ARIMA seasonal adjustment program can be found in "X-12-ARIMA Reference Manual, Version 0.3, February 28, 2011" at http://www.census.gov/srd/www/x12a/. The filter is implemented in IRIS (an open-source toolbox for MATLAB), which can be obtained from http://code.google.com/p/iris-toolbox-project/.
[9] Stock and Watson (2003, p. 803) report the same phenomenon in their study of international data.

For many countries, our sample encompasses periods over which recorded prices levels were likely distorted by nonmarket forces, like government price controls and major changes in indirect taxes.[10] Section 3 will discuss these episodes, and their effects on our estimates, in more detail. An overview of these dates is given in Table 2.

[Table 2 about here]

3. Model Description

Our paper uses two different models to estimate measures of trend levels and variability and to construct inflation forecasts. Both models are time-series models that use the same trend concept. The models mainly differ in the data on which their estimates are conditioned. The first model is the univariate UCSV model of Stock and Watson (2007, 2010), which is applied to data for each country's CPI inflation (headline). The second model is a variant of the multivariate common-trend model of Mertens (2011), which we estimate using data on three inflation series for each country, employing headline and core CPI as well as changes in the GDP deflator. As detailed below, both models use the trend concept of Beveridge and Nelson (1981), and both allow for time-varying volatility in trend shocks. The UCSV model embeds the assumption that deviations between actual inflation and trend have no persistence, whereas the multivariate model uses a (time-invariant) VAR to describe the dynamics of deviations between data and trend. While the UCSV model embeds two separate sources of stochastic volatility—one pertaining to trend shocks, the other to transitory shocks to inflation—only the trend shocks have stochastic volatility in the common-trend model.

Throughout this paper, we employ a Beveridge-Nelson (1981) decomposition of inflation into a trend level τ_t and inflation gap $\widetilde{\pi_t}$. As described presently, the two models used in this paper differ in their implied dynamics for the inflation gap. In both models, the Beveridge-Nelson trend measures each model's long-run forecast of inflation:

$$\pi_t = \tau_t + \widetilde{\pi_t} \qquad \tau_t = \lim_{k \to \infty} E_t \pi_{t+k}$$

---

[10] Some dates were excluded only from the GDP deflator series because of rebasing errors. The level series for Belgium, Canada, Germany, Italy, Spain and Switzerland all included large, discrete escalations in the price level that are not present in corresponding data reported in other studies such as Stock and Watson (2003). These data points are also not included in the analysis below of price shift dates. The dates removed from all estimations are 1966:Q1 (Italy), 1981:Q1 (Spain), 1991:Q1 (Germany), 1995:Q1 (Canada), and 1999:Q1 (Belgium and Spain).

Since the trend is defined as a martingale it follows a random walk driven by serially uncorrelated disturbances $\bar{e}_t$:

$$\tau_t = \tau_{t-1} + \bar{e}_t$$

This specification also imparts a random walk component to inflation. Whether this nonstationary component has relevant effects on observed inflation dynamics depends on the relative size of variations in trend and inflation gap. Our desideratum is that the estimates are well suited to environments in which inflation expectations are well anchored and trend changes are near-zero as well as episodes where expectations became unhinged and trend changes were large. To this end, the random walk disturbances are assumed to have stochastic volatility, with drifting log-variances, following the specification used, for example, by Stock and Watson (2007) as well as Cogley and Sargent (2005).

$$\bar{e}_t \sim N(0, \bar{\sigma}_t^2) \qquad \log \bar{\sigma}_t^2 = h_t = h_{t-1} + \varphi_h \xi_t \qquad \xi_t \sim N(0,1). \qquad (1)$$

This trend definition is then embedded into two models of inflation dynamics, to which we now turn.

Univariate UCSV Model

The UCSV model of Stock and Watson (2007) takes inflation as exhibiting no persistence and that it is also affected by a separate process for stochastic volatility:

$$\tilde{\pi}_t \sim N(0, \tilde{\sigma}_t^2) \qquad \log \tilde{\sigma}_t^2 = \tilde{h}_t = \tilde{h}_{t-1} + \varphi_{\tilde{h}} \tilde{\xi}_t \quad \tilde{\xi}_t \sim N(0,1).$$

Disturbances to trend and cycle, as well as the shocks to stochastic volatility, are assumed to be serially and mutually uncorrelated.

Multivariate Model (MVSV)

As an alternative to the univariate UCSV model, we also study trend estimates derived from a multivariate model with stochastic volatility (MVSV), which jointly conditions on three inflation measures for each country; a variant of the model has been applied by Mertens (2011) to U.S. data. Moreover, our model incorporates time-varying volatility in both the trend and the gap component of inflation. The model thus nests the UCSV case. In our application, the model uses observations on inflation in headline CPI, core CPI, and the GDP deflator, stacked into a vector Y_t, and applies a Beveridge-Nelson decomposition, similar to the UCSV model above:

$$Y_t = \tau_t + \tilde{Y}_t \qquad \tau_t = \lim_{k \to \infty} E_t Y_{t+k}$$

The key assumption of the multivariate model is that all variables in Y_t share the same common trend and their trend levels differ only up to a constant.[11] Crucially, trend changes in all three inflation measures are driven by a single shock, which has the same stochastic volatility behavior as in equation (1) above.

By contrast with the UCSV model, inflation gaps can be persistent in the multivariate model, provided they remain stationary. Specifically, the inflation gaps follow a stationary VAR with constant parameters and constant correlations and a common volatility factor:

$$A(L)\tilde{Y}_t = \tilde{e}_t \qquad \tilde{e}_t \sim N(0, \tilde{\sigma}_t^2 \Sigma)$$

The time-varying scale factor of the gap shocks is assumed to follow the same process as in the UCSV model; a random walk without drift in the log of $\tilde{\sigma}_t^2$. This approach has been proposed by Carriero et al. (2012), in the context of VARs applied to observable data instead of our inflation gaps. These authors report considerable gains—not only in computational efficiency but also model fit and forecast accuracy—from restricting the number of time-varying volatility factors this way, as opposed to assuming separate sources of stochastic volatility for each variable. In our application, such a more general specification even proved hard to implement, with at times hardly plausible results, likely due to the VAR being applied to the latent gap factors (as opposed to observable data), and the presence of missing data for several inflation series in many countries.

The roots of the VAR polynomial $A(L)$ are required to lie outside the unit circle, to ensure that the gaps are stationary. Shocks to gaps and trend are assumed to be mutually uncorrelated.[12] The multivariate thus nests the UCSV model, while extending it to multiple input series and

---

[11] Within the vector Y_t, average trend levels are allowed to differ to accommodate different average levels for the various inflation series.

[12] Mertens (2011) allows shocks to trend and gaps to be correlated. For simplicity, however, orthogonality is imposed here; for some countries the implied assumption of time-varying trend volatility but constant correlation between shocks to trend and gaps made the model hard to estimate.

persistent gap dynamics. Treating gap dynamics as time-invariant makes it easier for the model to handle a dataset, like ours, for which some series are missing or have missing observations.

Missing observations in Y_t are easily handled, by casting the model in state space form with (deterministic) time-variation in measurement loadings. In the case of missing observations, the appropriate elements of Y_t are encoded as zeros and so are their loadings on the model's states; see, for example, Mertens (2011) for details.

Estimation methods

The models are estimated with Markov-Chain Monte Carlo methods, as described in Mertens (2011). The algorithm yields not only estimates of the latent factors. The sampling algorithm recovers the posterior distribution of missing data entries, conditional on the model and all observed data values. Convergence is assessed with scale reduction tests, applied to the output of multiple chains that started from dispersed initial conditions.

4. Inflation Trends: Levels and Uncertainty

This section reports country-by-country estimates of inflation trends and gaps as well as their time-varying variability, generated from the UCSV model of Stock and Watson (2007) and our MVSV model. The UCSV estimates complement and extend the results reported by Cecchetti, Hooper, Kasman, Schoenholtz, and Watson (2007), whose estimates are conditioned on the GDP deflators for the G7 countries. The UCSV estimates reported below are conditioned on CPI inflation (headline). For ease of comparison, we also report only the gap estimates of CPI (headline) inflation for the MVSV model.[13] The estimates reported below are conditioned on all available data from 1960:Q1 through 2012:Q4, except for the removal of certain dates, listed in Table 2, when price shifts occurred. The nature of these price shifts and their effect on our estimates are discussed in Section 5.

[Figures 1–14 about here]

Comparing estimates from the UCSV model and the MVSV for each country, there are some broad similarities, but also notable differences. Estimates from both models capture very similar

---

[13] Gap estimates for core CPI and the GDP deflator will be provided in a separate appendix.

low-frequency movements. But, typically, the trend estimates from the UCSV model are more variable, and comove more strongly with the actual data, while the gap estimates of the UCSV model are much less persistent. Compared with the MVSV estimates, the UCSV trend estimates appear to overstate changes in trend inflation by several percentage points. Similarly, there are marked differences in the stochastic volatility estimates from both models. While estimates from both models typically imply a decline in trend volatility over the postwar sample, the UCSV estimates generally suggest a much greater degree of unanchored inflation expectations in the 1970s, while MVSV estimates of trend volatility display a much milder hump shape, if not a mere gradual decline in most countries. One striking feature is that much of the time variation in UCSV estimates of trend volatility seems to be captured by time-variation in the MVSV estimates of gap volatility.

Several countries, listed in the lower panel of Table 1, have introduced formal inflation goals during the sample period. In most cases, estimated trend levels from both models tend to hover around these goals. However, there are also some notable differences, discussed further below. After the formal introduction of an inflation target, our measure of anchored inflation expectations—the stochastic volatility of trend shocks—decreases in many cases only within about five to ten years, reflecting the fact that our measure is conditioned solely on the realized inflation history in a given country.

Amidst the countries with explicit inflation goals, the trend estimates for Sweden, shown in Panels (a) and (b) of Figure 11, stand out, as the trend is almost permanently hovering about half a percentage point below the Riksbank's inflation target of 2%, consistent with Svensson's (2013) characterization of inflation expectations in Sweden. Similarly, inflation trend estimates for Germany (shown in Figure 5) are running almost 1 percentage point below the ECB's target rate of "close to but below 2%," while trend estimates for other Eurozone countries are typically much closer to 2%.

An interesting comparison between the MVSV and UCSV estimates is offered by the case of the United Kingdom, estimates for which are displayed in Table 13. Over recent years, U.K. inflation has been persistently running above the Bank of England's 2% target, and these overshoots have some influence on our estimates. In particular, the UCSV estimates are increasing over the last five years, up to levels near 4%. In contrast, the MVSV model implies a more limited and tentative increase in trend inflation for the United Kingdom because of persistence embedded into the model specification of gap dynamics.

The estimated trend levels for Japan, shown in Figure 8, are amongst the lowest in our cross-country sample. Both MVSV and UCSV estimates put trend inflation for Japan at levels below zero for the last decade and in particular the 90% credible sets of the MVSV model barely cover any positive values over that period. Concerns about rising deflation risks are also raised by our trend estimates for Switzerland, shown in Figure 12, which have clearly been drifting toward zero over the last few years, having remained stable near two percent for most of the last 15 years.

5. The Effects of Price Shift Dates on Trend Estimates

The estimates presented in the previous section are conditioned on all available data in our sample, except for the removal of country-specific dates on which price shifts occurred due to nonmarket factors.[14] The results shown in Figures 1 to 14 were generated from inflation data for which periods of price shifts are treated as missing values in each model's estimation. The relevance of these episodes for our estimates, including a comparison with estimates conditional on all data, is the subject of this section.

All in all, we consider 15 price shift episodes affecting 7 out of the 14 countries in our sample; all are listed in Table 2. Most episodes are related to increases in taxes on goods and services and similar administrative surcharges, thus removing only a single quarterly observation from the data. The rationale for omitting these specific dates is that the price level shifted in the period in question not as a reflection of monetary policy or of private sector-initiated behavior, but because of a nonmonetary governmental measure whose effect was essentially to rescale the price level. Only three episodes were somewhat longer: The price controls in the United States (1971–1974) and New Zealand (1982–1984) as well as the transition period in the wake of German reunification (1991). Again, the shift in the price level in these dates corresponded either to a movement away from market determination of prices (in the case of the price control

---

[14] Inflation data for periods of price shifts are treated as missing values in the estimation.

episodes) or a major redefinition of the area covered by the price index (as when the former East Germany was brought into the Federal Republic of Germany).[15]

[Figure 15 about here]

Reflecting their short duration, the price shift dates leave not much impact on trend estimates for many countries. But this is not invariably the case. Figure 15 presents trend estimates for four countries, German, Ireland, New Zealand and the U.S., for which the inclusion of price shift dates has nonnegligible effect on trend estimates, at least when using the UCSV model. The figure compares the trend estimates discussed in the previous section against estimates that condition on the entire data, including inflation data recorded during the price shift episodes. For each country, trend estimates from the MVSV around the price shift dates are not much affected whether the price shift data is included or excluded from the estimation. However, there are however sizable differences in the case of the UCSV estimates. For example, the UCSV estimate of trend inflation in the U.S. peaks above 10% in the mid-1970s, when conditioned on the full data, whereas in the case where the price shifts are treated as missing data, the estimated inflation trend rises only gradually from about 5 to 8 percent during the same period.

Also, the estimated gap volatilities from the UCSV model prove to be more sensitive to the inclusion of price shift dates in the case of the U.S., and the same is true for New Zealand (see Panel (h) of Figures 9 and 14). In both cases, UCSV estimates of the gap levels right before and after the price shift periods are notably elevated, consistent with a rise in volatility. When the price shifts are treated as missing data, the random walk assumption then causes the estimated volatilities to remain elevated throughout the price shift period, whereas these patterns are somewhat mollified when all data are included (results not shown here).

[Figures 16–17 about here]

Detailed results for each country, with and without price shift dates are provided in Figure 16 (for the MVSV model) and Figure 17 (for the UCSV model).

---

[15] Gordon (1983) and Staiger, Stock, and Watson (1997) are previous studies that allowed for the effects of price controls in their study of inflation dynamics, while Levin and Piger (2004) allow for major changes in national sales taxes. In addition, the exclusion of control and tax periods from the estimates represents a step in the direction of incorporating historical information about individual countries' experiences into the study of inflation dynamics, as recommended by Cecchetti, Hooper, Kasman, Schoenholtz, and Watson (2007).

6. Trend Estimates in Real Time

The trend estimates described in the previous two sections have been conditioned on full sample data—with or without price shifts. Such estimates are typically also called "smoothed" estimates, as opposed to "filtered" estimates, which condition trend estimates for time t only onto data up to time t. This section describes filtered estimates of trend inflation.

The filtered estimates presented here, are derived from a real-time analysis, where each model has been re-estimated for each quarter from 1984:Q4 through 2012:Q4.[16] The difference between filtered and smoothed estimates incorporates thus also the effects of re-estimating the model's hyperparameters like φ_h, governing the volatility of shocks to the stochastic log-variances, or the coefficients $A(L)$ of the gap VAR. Before analyzing each model's forecast performance based on this real-time analysis, this section first compares smoothed and filtered estimates of trend inflation from the MVSV model, as well as the difference between filtered estimates of trend inflation between the UCSV and the MVSV model.

Our discussion is limited here to a subset of countries, for which the comparison brings out some particular differences between filtered and smoothed estimates. These countries are Australia, Canada, New Zealand, Sweden and the United Kingdom, and each of them is characterized by a disinflation period, preceding the formal adoption of an inflation targeting regime. (Results for all countries are shown in a separate appendix.)

[Figure 18 about here]

The left-hand panels of Figure 18 compare filtered and smoothed estimates from the MVSV model for these countries. Not surprisingly, the filtered estimates for each country are less smooth than their smoothed counterparts. (This is also true for results from the other countries shown in the appendix.) There are, however, remarkably persistent differences between filtered and smoothed estimates in years ahead of (and to some extent also after) the adoption of an inflation target for the countries shown in Figure 18. For these countries, inflation has been several percentage points above the subsequently adopted target levels ten years prior to their targeting regimes. Consequently, the smoothed estimates typically display a gradual decrease in

---

[16] Strictly speaking, this is only a *pseudo*-real-time analysis, since we abstract from data revisions and the exact publication dates for each inflation series.

trend inflation that often starts well before the formal adoption of inflation targeting. In contrast, the filtered estimates typically begin to decrease later and less gradually, and closer to the actual begin of the targeting regime.

Mechanically, this behavior is, of course, exactly what smoothed and filtered estimates are designed to deliver. While smoothed estimates are designed to be more precise estimates of the underlying inflation trend, they also benefit from hindsight knowledge about realized inflation at later dates, and they may thus not lend themselves to exercises such as determining the exact timing of events like the introduction of an inflation target. The filtered estimates might thus be more suitable for comparison against other measures of trend inflation derived from financial market indicators.

Filtered estimates from the UCSV and the MVSV model are shown in the right-hand side panels of Figure 18. These figures are thus analogous to what is shown in Panels (a) and (b) of Figures 1 through 14 for the smoothed estimates. While the filtered estimates are generally a bit more variable than their smoothed counterparts, the general message from comparing the trend estimates of the UCSV model and the MVSV model is the same as before: The UCSV estimates of the inflation trend take at times undue signal from transitory movements in the inflation data, and this phenomenon is visible in the figure as swings in the UCSV trend around the corresponding MVSV estimates.

7. Forecast Evaluation

Trend inflation is a latent and unobservable variable. Arguably, the MVSV estimates documented in the previous sections might appear more appealing than their UCSV counterparts—on the grounds, for example, that the UCSV estimates appear to be influenced by transitory changes in inflation. But such a conclusion relies more on a subjective impression of what constitutes a "reasonable" estimate rather than a direct comparison between estimates and actual values of trend inflation, which is however infeasible to do. An indirect way to assess the validity or usefulness of different trend estimates would be to evaluate inflation forecasts generated by each model at some finite horizons. As the Beveridge-Nelson trend answers a forecasting problem, the idea behind this approach is that a good trend model should be good at forecasting, and probably also at shorter horizons. Evaluating the forecast performance of different trend models may then not only be interesting in order to assess different trend estimates, but should also be relevant for researchers who are especially concerned with generating good inflation forecasts. As argued by Faust and Wright (2012), good inflation forecasts are typically centered on a good trend measure.

This section evaluates inflation forecasts up to four years ahead derived from the UCSV and MVSV model for each country. In addition, we also consider forecasts derived from the random walk benchmark of Atkinson and Ohanian (2001); in this case, inflation forecasts for all horizons are set equal to a four-quarter moving average of lagged inflation. Inflation forecasts are generated in (pseudo-) real time from 1985 onwards. The first forecast is thus conditioned on model estimates obtained for data from 1960:Q1 through 1984:Q4, with an increasing estimation window as the forecast period moves forward. Each quarter, inflation forecasts are generated both for annual inflation rates (computed as the average of expected inflation rates over four consecutive quarters) as well as quarterly changed at different horizons.[17] Annual inflation rates are forecasted for the upcoming four quarters, one year ahead (quarters 5–8), two years ahead (quarters 9–12), three years ahead (quarters 13–16) and four years ahead (quarters 17–20); quarterly inflation rates are forecasted for the next quarter, then 4, 8, 12 and 16 quarters ahead. Results are fairly insensitive to the inclusion of the price shift dates discussed in Section 5— which mostly occurred prior to our forecast window ranging from 1985 to 2012—and all results are derived from data which includes the price shift dates.

[Tables 3 and 4 about here]

Forecast accuracy is measured here with root-mean-squared errors ("RMSE"), which are reported in Table 3 for forecasts of annual inflation and Table 4 for quarterly inflation rates; in both cases inflation rates are expressed as annualized percentage rates. In Tables 3 and 4, forecast performance of alternative models is measured by the ratio of each model's RMSE compared to the MVSV model. A value below unity indicates that the MVSV model has a lower

---

[17] Stock and Watson (2009) also focus on forecasts of one-year or even two-year price changes, whereas Faust and Wright study forecasts of quarterly inflation rates.

RMSE, and conversely for values above unity. The statistical significance of th difference from unity of these values is assessed with the Diebold and Mariano (1995) test.[18]

Several results are common to both tables. First, the MVSV model generates lower RMSE for each country and at each horizon than a simple random walk forecast. Second, in most countries, the same is also true when the MVSV forecasts are compared against the UCSV model; however to a lesser extent. For a few countries however, notably France, Italy and Spain, the MVSV model delivers consistently worse RMSE than the UCSV model. Third, while most of these differences are quite sizeable—in the order of one or two tenths of the MVSV model's RMSE—they are often not statistically significant. Mainly for the longer-horizon forecasts of inflation in Japan, Switzerland and the United States does the MVSV model produce forecasts that are significantly better than projections derived from a random walk or the UCSV model. Strikingly, the MVSV model does never significantly worse than its competitors.

Comparing the absolute levels of the RMSE for the MVSV model between both tables shows that RMSE levels are somewhat larger when trying to forecast quarterly rather than annual inflation rates. This pattern is indicative of a nontrivial amount of highly transitory—and thus harder to forecast—fluctuations found in quarterly data, which are less prevalent when trying to forecast annual inflation. As a corollary, the relative differences in RMSE between the different models reported in Table 4 are also smaller in size and tend to be less significant as in the case of the annual inflation forecasts reported in Table 3.

As a final comparison, we also consider the forecasting performance of the MVSV trend alone, neglecting the horizon specific information resulting from the VAR component of the model's gap equation (for a given trend estimate). In this case, forecasts for all horizons are set equal to the models trend estimate, generated in real time, and as plotted in Figure 18. Apart from further underscoring the value of the embedding persistence into the model's gap equation, this comparison also brings out an important distinction between forecasting annual versus quarterly inflation rates. Considering projections for quarterly inflation, reported in Table 4, there is not much of a difference between the average forecast errors of the MVSV model (including the gap

---

[18] The Diebold Mariano (1995) test checks whether the squared losses generated by two different forecasts are, on average, equal. Reflecting the overlap in the forecast periods, the standard errors are computed using the Newey and West (1997) HAC estimator with a bandwidth equal to one plus the forecast horizon.

forecast) and projections derived from the MVSV trend alone. This finding is consistent with the notion that most of the forecast accuracy of the MVSV model stems from the quality of its trend forecasts, and that the model's VAR equation for the inflation gap does not add much value beyond shaping the trend estimate itself. However, when the forecast comparison for the annual rates is considered (see Table 4), a different picture emerges: In this case, the forecasts from the MVSV model significantly outperform the MVSV trend in forecasting inflation in virtually every case, and mostly at high significance levels. This result strongly supports the notion that there is important value in embedding persistence in the model's gap equation, which has already been evident in the comparison of the trend estimates described in Section 4. However, when considering projections of quarterly inflation instead of annual rates the contribution to forecast accuracy of the horizon-specific gap forecast seems to be swamped by the quarterly noise in inflation.

8. Conclusion

Our paper compares estimates of trend inflation in fourteen advanced economies using two different models. Our preferred model is a multivariate extension to Stock and Watson's (2007) the unobserved components model with stochastic volatility (UCSV) that has been applied to the G7 countries by Cecchetti, Hooper, Kasman, Schoenholtz, and Watson (2007). Like the UCSV model, our multivariate stochastic volatility model (MVSV) tracks time-variation in the variability of shocks to trend inflation and inflation gap. Gap estimates from our model display persistence, while the UCSV model embeds the assumption that gaps are serially uncorrelated. The MVSV trends are consequently smoother and less variable, since the underlying filtering procedure exhibits less leakage from persistent components of the data, which do not prove to be permanent. Thus, the MVSV estimates are less influenced by the occurrence of country-specific episodes in which price levels shifted because of non-market factors, like tax changes.

In addition, the MVSV model conditions on multiple inflation series, assuming they share a common trend as in the model of Mertens (2011). In contrast to Cogley and Sargent (2005) and Cogley, Primiceri, and Sargent (2010), our model restricts time-variation in its parameters only to stochastic volatility, and to have only two sources: drift in the log-variances of shocks to the common trend and a common scale factor to all gaps. Placing a limit in this way on the amount of time-varying parameters makes the model more tractable, and it also enables us to handle missing data in some of the inflation series for several countries. This restricted approach also holds out the prospect of better forecast accuracy. Compared to simple random walk forecasts—generated either from a trailing 4-quarter moving average or the UCSV model—our MVSV model typically reduces the average size of forecast errors at many horizons and for most countries. In particular, for the exercise of forecasting four-quarter inflation rates (as opposed to quarterly rates), the improvements are quite sizeable. However, overall it remains hard to outperform these benchmark forecasts with statistical significance.

While our estimates of trend inflation display quite some similarities across countries—notably the shared experiences of persistently elevated inflation rates during the 1970s and more reliably-anchored inflation expectations over the last two decades—there are also clear differences in the trend estimates. For example, the extent to which trend inflation rose and fell over the postwar sample differs markedly across countries. Also, for many countries, distinct, country-specific changes in monetary regime, like the adoption of a formal inflation target, are clearly visible in the trend estimates.

References

Atkenson, A. and L. E. Ohanian. (2001, Winter). Are Phillips curves useful for forecasting inflation? *Quarterly Review 25*(1), 2-11.

Beveridge, S. and C. R. Nelson (1981). A new approach to decomposition of economic time series into permanent and transitory components with particular attention to measurement of the "business cycle". *Journal of Monetary Economics 7*(2), 151-174.

Carriero, A., T. E. Clark, and M. Marcellino (2012). Common drifting volatility in large Bayesian vars. Working Paper 1206, Federal Reserve Bank of Cleveland.

Cecchetti, S. G., P. Hooper, B. C. Kasman, K. L. Schoenholtz, and M. W. Watson (2007, July). Understanding the evolving inflation process. U.S. Monetary Policy Forum on March 9, 2007, sponsored by the Initiative on Global Markets at the University of Chicago Booth School of Business (revised version).

Ciccarelli, M. and B. Mojon (2010, August). Global inflation. *The Review of Economics and Statistics 92*(3), 524-535.

Clark, T. E. and T. Doh (2011, December). A Bayesian evaluation of alternative models of trend inflation. Working Paper 1134, Federal Reserve Bank of Cleveland.

Cogley, T., G. E. Primiceri, and T. J. Sargent (2010, January). Inflation-gap persistence in the U.S. *American Economic Journal: Macroeconomics 2*(1), 43-69.

Cogley, T. and T. J. Sargent (2005, April). Drift and volatilities: Monetary policies and outcomes in the post WWII U.S. *Review of Economic Dynamics 8*(2), 262-302.

Cogley, T., T. J. Sargent, and P. Surico (2013, January). Price-level uncertainty and stability in the U.K. *mimeo*.

Cogley, T. and A. M. Sbordone (2008, December). Trend inflation, indexation, and inflation persistence in the New Keynesian Phillips curve. *The American Economic Review 98*(5), 2101-26.

Diebold, F. X. and R. S. Mariano (1995, July). Comparing predictive accuracy. *Journal of Business & Economic Statistics 13*(3), 253-63.

Faust, J. and J. H. Wright (2012, June). Forecasting inflation. *mimeo*, Department of Economics, Johns Hopkins University.

Frye, J. and R. J. Gordon (1981, May). Government intervention in the inflation process: The econometrics of "Self-Inflicted Wounds". *American Economic Review 71*(2), 288-94.

Gordon, R. J. (1983, May). Wages and prices are not always sticky: A century of evidence for the United States, United Kingdom, and Japan. NBER Working Papers 0847, National Bureau of Economic Research, Inc.

Ireland, P. N. (2007, December). Changes in the Federal Reserve's inflation target: Causes and consequences. *Journal of Money, Credit and Banking 39*(8), 1851-1882.

Kozicki, S. and P. Tinsley (2012, 02). Effective use of survey information in estimating the evolution of expected inflation. *Journal of Money, Credit and Banking 44*(1), 145-169.

Levin, A. T. and J. M. Piger (2004, April). Is inflation persistence intrinsic in industrial economies? Working Paper Series 334, European Central Bank.

Mertens, E (2011). Measuring the level of uncertainty of trend inflation. *Finance and Economics Discussion Series 42*. Board of Governors of the Federal Reserve System.

Mishkin, F. S. (2007). Inflation dynamics. *International Finance 10*, 317-334.

Neiss, K. S. and E. Nelson (2005). Inflation dynamics, marginal cost, and the output gap: Evidence from three countries. *Journal of Money, Credit and Banking 37*(6), pp. 1019-1045.

Newey, W. and K. West (1987). A simple positive semi-definite heteroskedasticity and autocorrelation consistent covariance matrix. *Econometrica 55*, 703-708.

Staiger, D. O., J. H. Stock, and M. W. Watson (1997). How precise are estimates of the natural rate of unemployment? In *Reducing Inflation: Motivation and Strategy*, NBER Chapters, Chapter 5, pp. 195-246. National Bureau of Economic Research, Inc.

Stock, J. H. and M. W. Watson (2007). Why Has U.S. Inflation Become Harder to Forecast? *Journal of Money, Credit and Banking* 39(1), pp. 13-33.

Stock, J. H. and M. W. Watson (2009, September). Phillips curve inflation forecasts. In J. Fuhrer, Y. K. Kodrzycki, J. S. Little, and G. P. Olivei (Eds.), *Understanding Inflation and the Implications for Monetary Policy – A Phillips Curve Retrospective*, Chapter 3, pp. 99-184. Cambridge, MA: MIT Press.

Stock, J. H. and M. W. Watson (2010, October). Modeling inflation after the crisis. NBER Working Papers 16488, National Bureau of Economic Research, Inc.

Stock, J. H. and M. W. Watson (2003, September). Forecasting output and inflation: The role of asset prices. *Journal of Economic Literature 41*(3), 788-829.

Svensson, L. E. O. (2013, April). The possible unemployment cost of average inflation below a credible target. *mimeo*.

Wright, J. H. (2011, September). Term premia and inflation uncertainty: Empirical evidence from an international panel dataset. *American Economic Review 101*(4), 1514-34.

List of Figures

1	Australia	2
2	Belgium	3
3	Canada	4
4	France	5
5	Germany	6
6	Ireland	7
7	Italy	8
8	Japan	9
9	New Zealand	10
10	Spain	11
11	Sweden	12
12	Switzerland	13
13	United Kingdom	14
14	United States	15
15	Trend Estimates and Price Shift Dates	16
16a	Trend Estimates for MVSV Model	17
16b	Trend Estimates for MVSV Model	18
17a	Trend Estimates for UCSV Model	19
17b	Trend Estimates for UCSV Model	20
18a	Filtered Trend Estimates	21
18b	Filtered Trend Estimates (ctd.)	22

List of Tables

1	Data Overview	23
2	Omitted Price Shift Dates	24
3	Forecast Evaluation: Annual Inflation Rates	25
4	Forecast Evaluation: Quarterly Inflation Rates	27

Figure 1: Australia

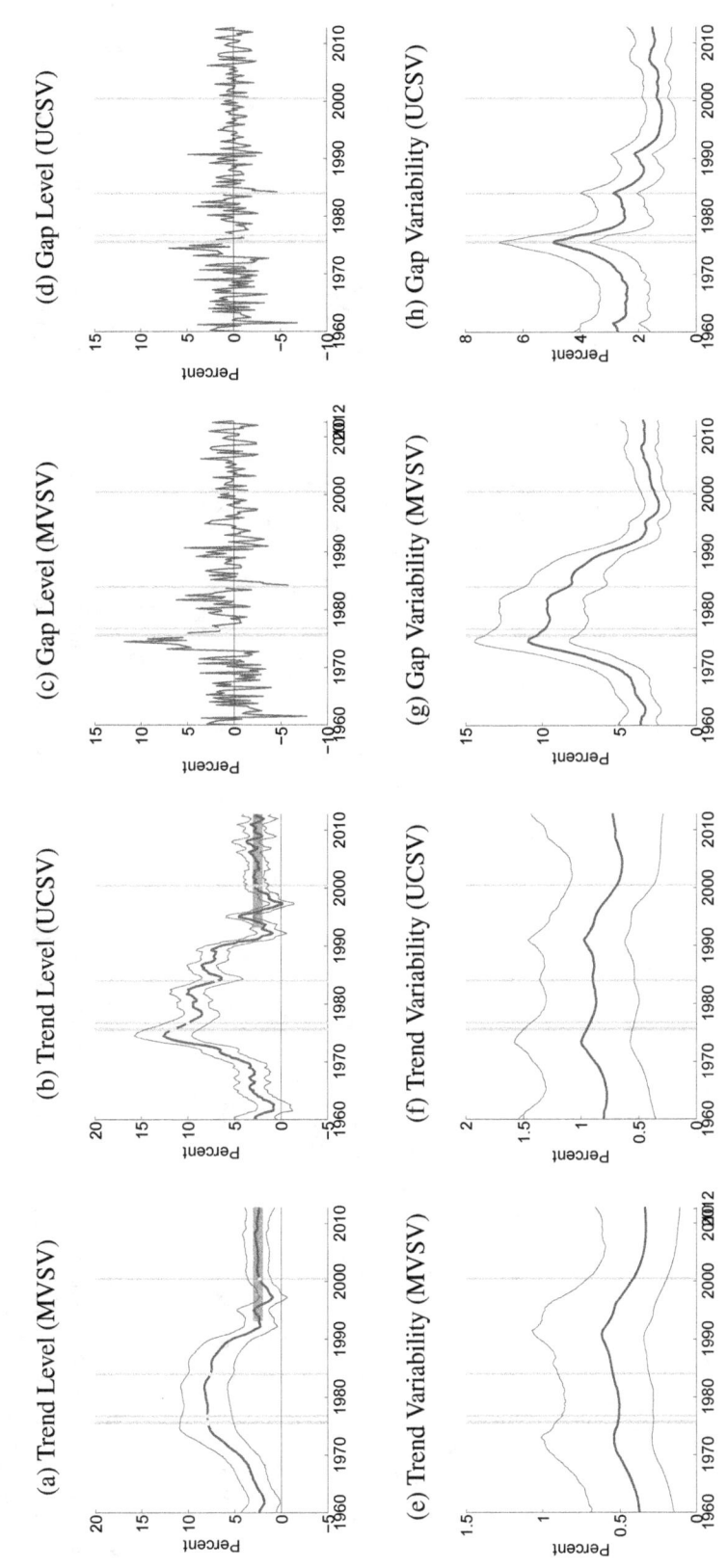

Note: Solid, thick blue lines show posterior means, and thinner blue lines depict 90% confidence sets derived from the model's posterior distribution conditional on all data. All levels are measured in annualized percentage points. Uncertainty is measured by the standard deviation of a quarterly trend shock. Data sources as listed in Table 1, using all available data since 1960. Grey shading marks dates in which data was excluded from computation due to shifts in the price index at that time. All country specific price shift dates for input measures are listed in Table 2. For those periods, estimated inflation gaps, shown in Panels (c) and (d), are marked green. When there are no price shift dates, the gap estimates are identical to the difference between actual inflation and the trend estimates, shown in Panels (a) and (b). In Panels (a) and (b), the solid red line marks the range of an offically stated inflation goal.

Figure 2: Belgium

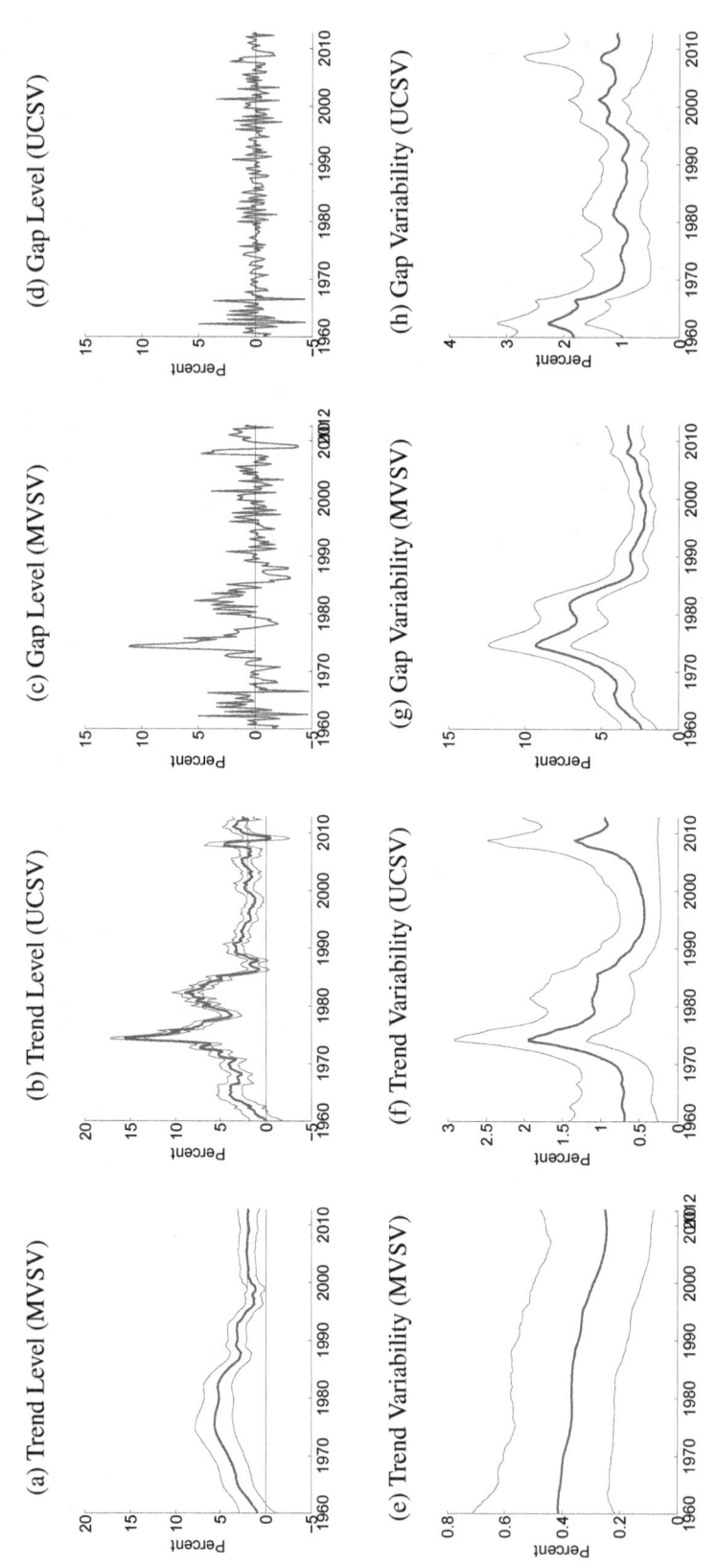

Note: Solid, thick blue lines show posterior means, and thinner blue lines depict 90% confidence sets derived from the model's posterior distribution conditional on all data. All levels are measured in annualized percentage points. Uncertainty is measured by the standard deviation of a quarterly trend shock. Data sources as listed in Table 1, using all available data since 1960. In Panels (a) and (b), the solid red line marks the level of an offically stated inflation goal.

Figure 3: Canada

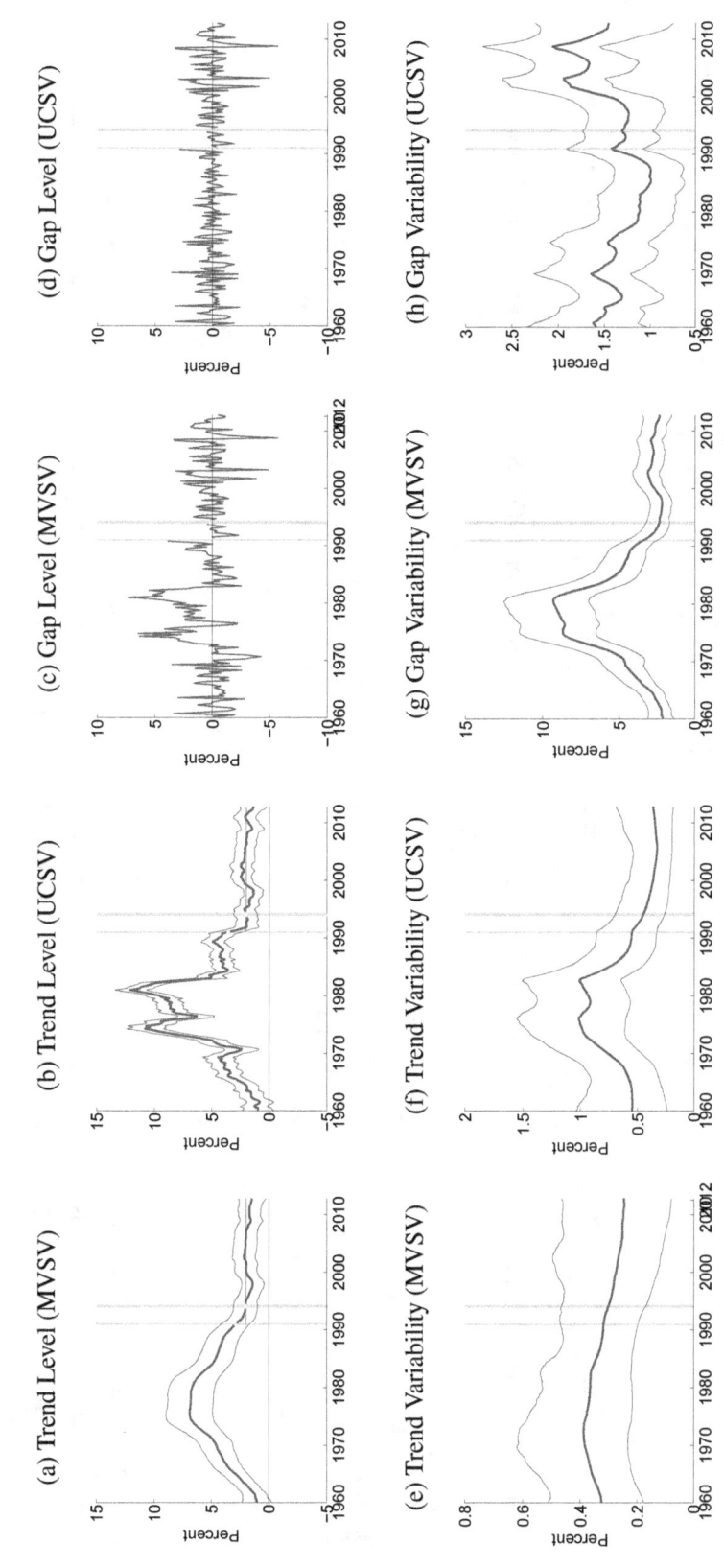

Note: Solid, thick blue lines show posterior means, and thinner blue lines depict 90% confidence sets derived from the model's posterior distribution conditional on all data. All levels are measured in annualized percentage points. Uncertainty is measured by the standard deviation of a quarterly trend shock. Data sources as listed in Table 1, using all available data since 1960. Grey shading marks dates in which data was excluded from computation due to shifts in the price index at that time. All country specific price shift dates for input measures are listed in Table 2. For those periods, estimated inflation gaps, shown in Panels (c) and (d), are marked green. When there are no price shift dates, the gap estimates are identical to the difference between actual inflation and the trend estimates, shown in Panels (a) and (b). In Panels (a) and (b), the solid red line marks the level of an offically stated inflation goal.

Figure 4: France

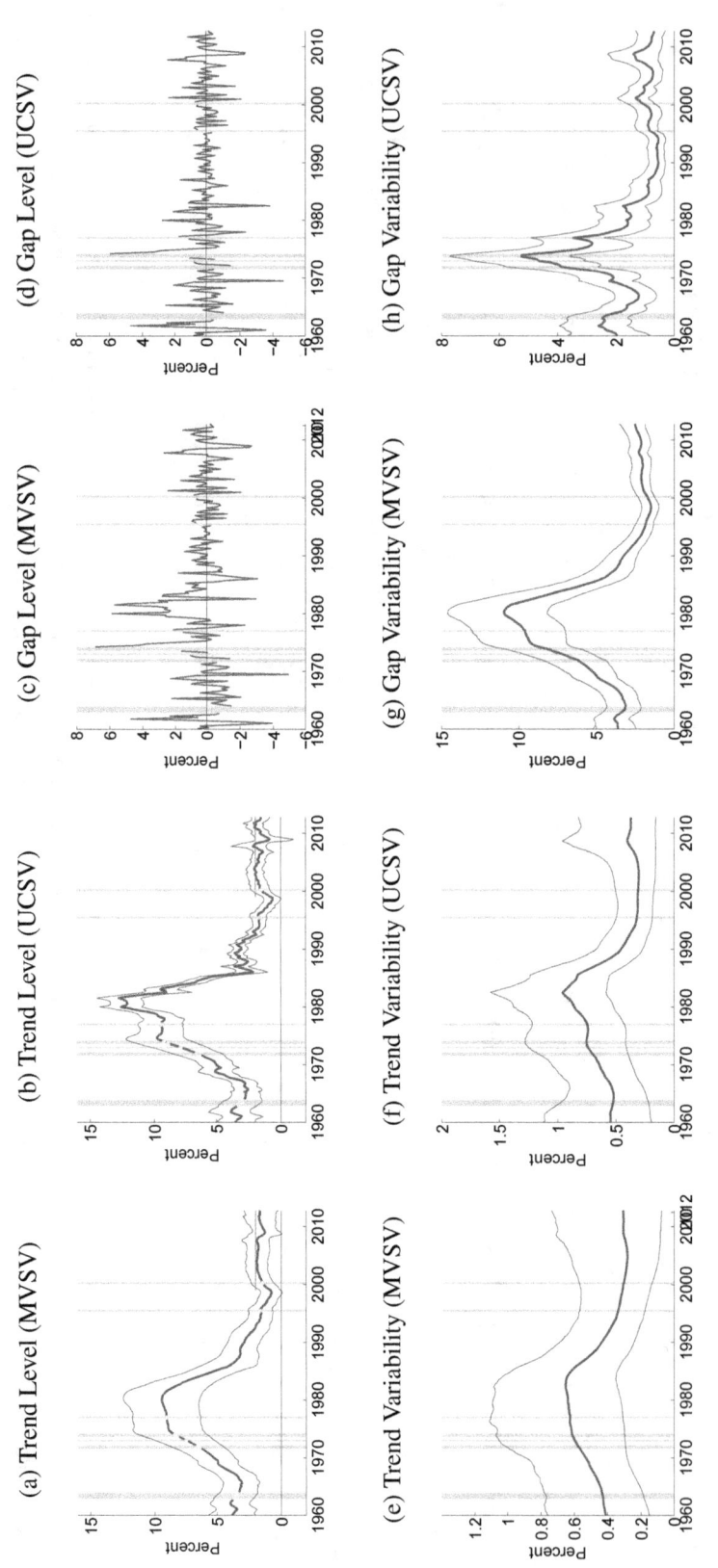

Note: Solid, thick blue lines show posterior means, and thinner blue lines depict 90% confidence sets derived from the model's posterior distribution conditional on all data. All levels are measured in annualized percentage points. Uncertainty is measured by the standard deviation of a quarterly trend shock. Data sources as listed in Table 1, using all available data since 1960. In Panels (a) and (b), the solid red line marks the level of an offically stated inflation goal.

Figure 5: Germany

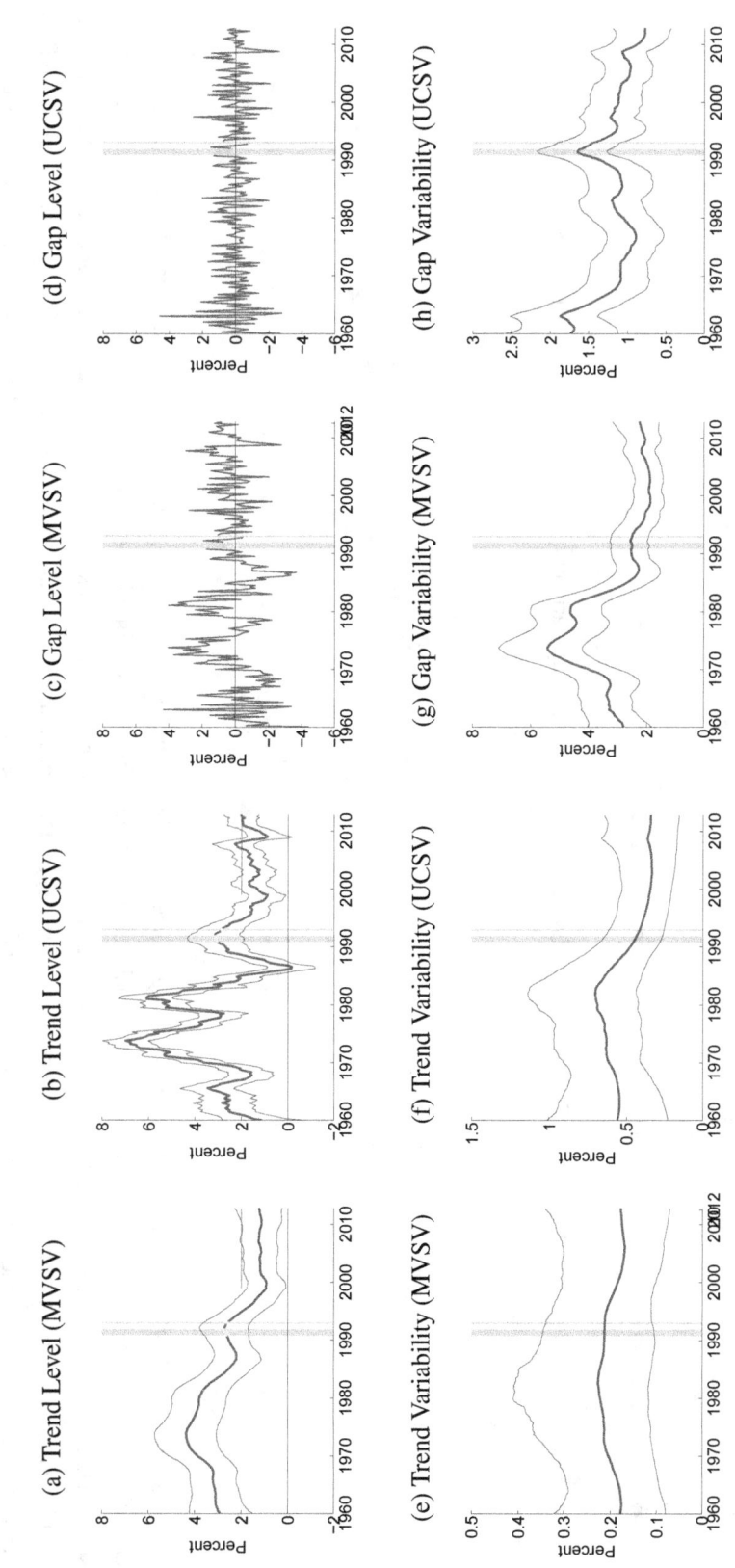

Note: Solid, thick blue lines show posterior means, and thinner blue lines depict 90% confidence sets derived from the model's posterior distribution conditional on all data. All levels are measured in annualized percentage points. Uncertainty is measured by the standard deviation of a quarterly trend shock. Data sources as listed in Table 1, using all available data since 1960. Grey shading marks dates in which data was excluded from computation due to shifts in the price index at that time. All country specific price shift dates for input measures are listed in Table 2. For those periods, estimated inflation gaps, shown in Panels (c) and (d), are marked green. When there are no price shift dates, the gap estimates are identical to the difference between actual inflation and the trend estimates, shown in Panels (a) and (b). In Panels (a) and (b), the solid red line marks the level of an offically stated inflation goal.

Figure 6: Ireland

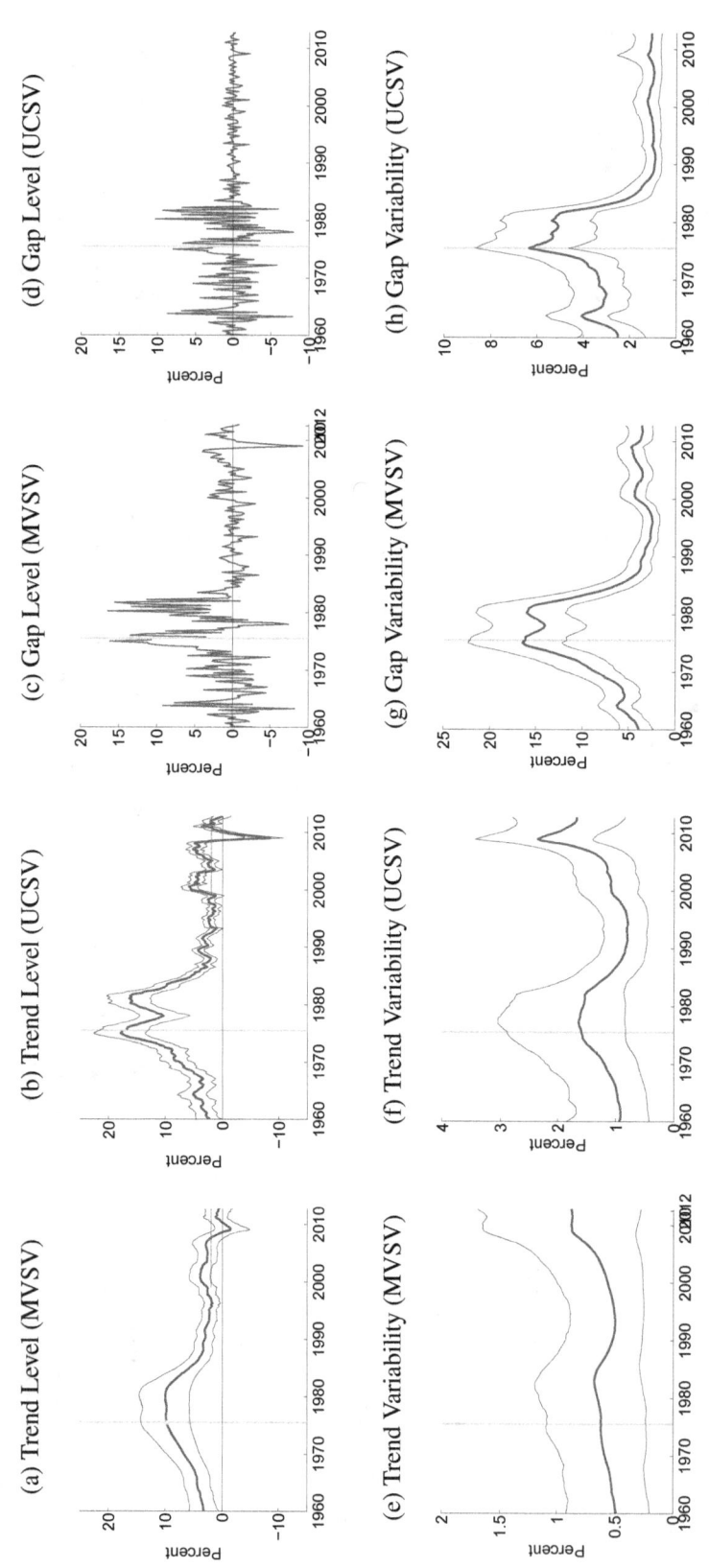

Note: Solid, thick blue lines show posterior means, and thinner blue lines depict 90% confidence sets derived from the model's posterior distribution conditional on all data. All levels are measured in annualized percentage points. Uncertainty is measured by the standard deviation of a quarterly trend shock. Data sources as listed in Table 1, using all available data since 1960. Grey shading marks dates in which data was excluded from computation due to shifts in the price index at that time. All country specific price shift dates for input measures are listed in Table 2. For those periods, estimated inflation gaps, shown in Panels (c) and (d), are marked green. When there are no price shift dates, the gap estimates are identical to the difference between actual inflation and the trend estimates, shown in Panels (a) and (b). In Panels (a) and (b), the solid red line marks the level of an offically stated inflation goal.

Figure 7: Italy

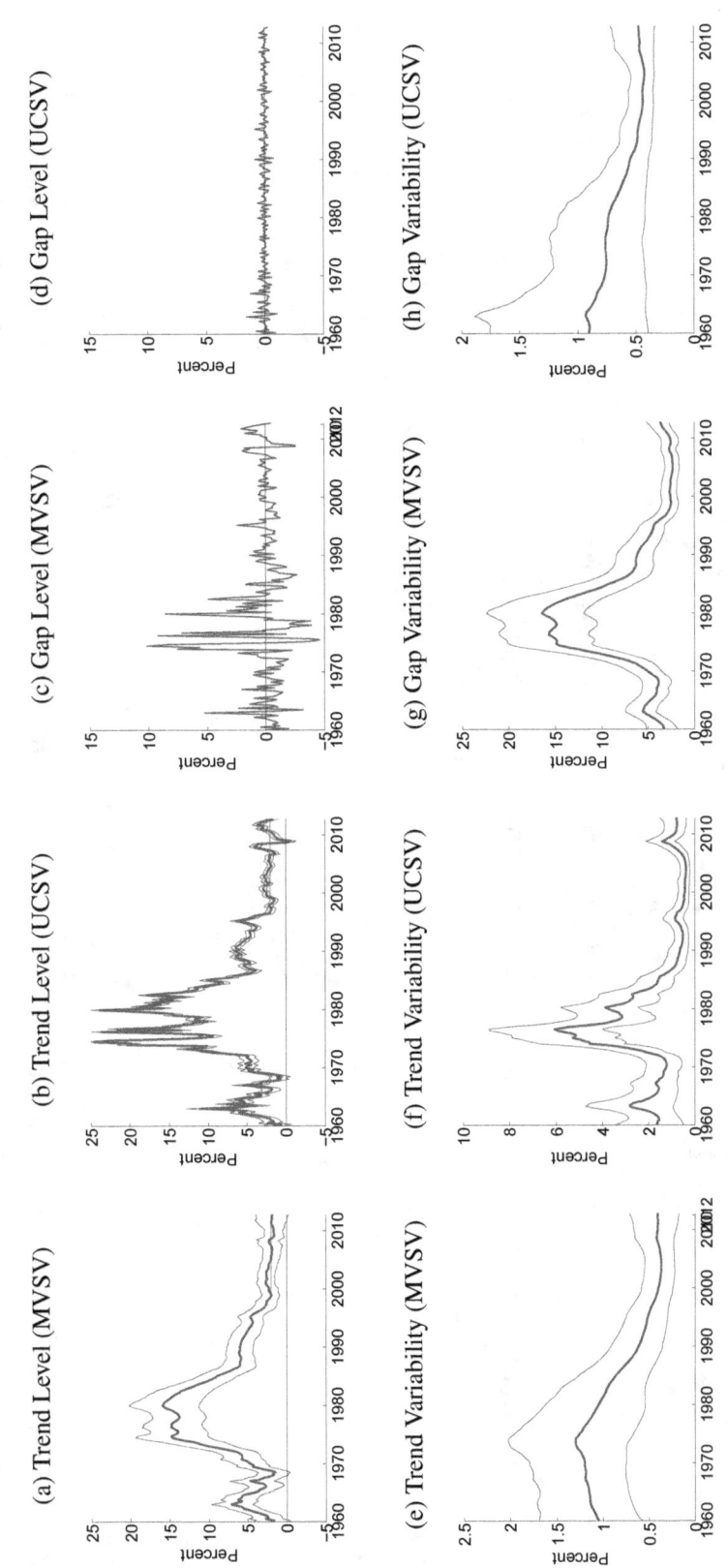

Note: Solid, thick blue lines show posterior means, and thinner blue lines depict 90% confidence sets derived from the model's posterior distribution conditional on all data. All levels are measured in annualized percentage points. Uncertainty is measured by the standard deviation of a quarterly trend shock. Data sources as listed in Table 1, using all available data since 1960. In Panels (a) and (b), the solid red line marks the level of an offically stated inflation goal.

Figure 8: Japan

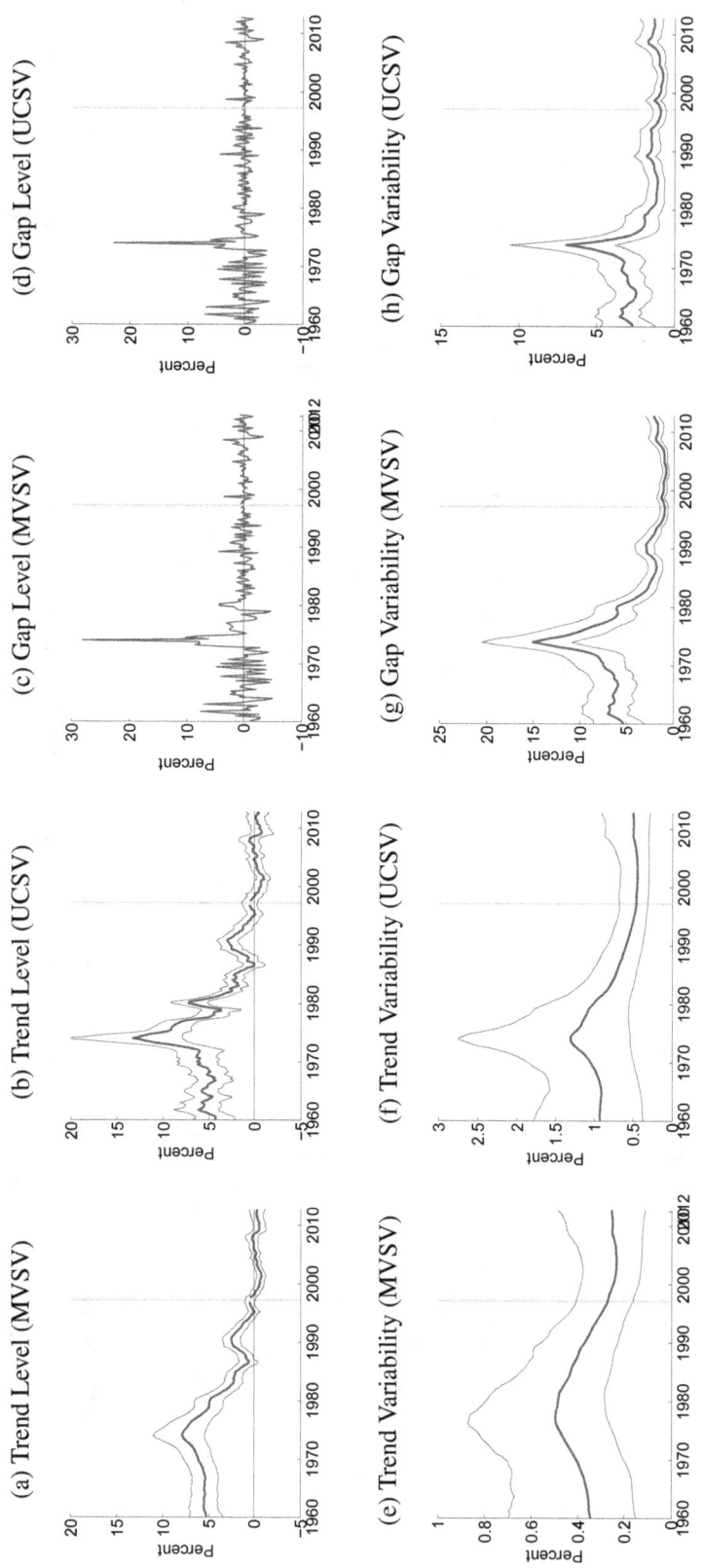

Note: Solid, thick blue lines show posterior means, and thinner blue lines depict 90% confidence sets derived from the model's posterior distribution conditional on all data. All levels are measured in annualized percentage points. Uncertainty is measured by the standard deviation of a quarterly trend shock. Data sources as listed in Table 1, using all available data since 1960. Grey shading marks dates in which data was excluded from computation due to shifts in the price index at that time. All country specific price shift dates for input measures are listed in Table 2. For those periods, estimated inflation gaps, shown in Panels (c) and (d), are marked green. When there are no price shift dates, the gap estimates are identical to the difference between actual inflation and the trend estimates, shown in Panels (a) and (b).

Figure 9: New Zealand

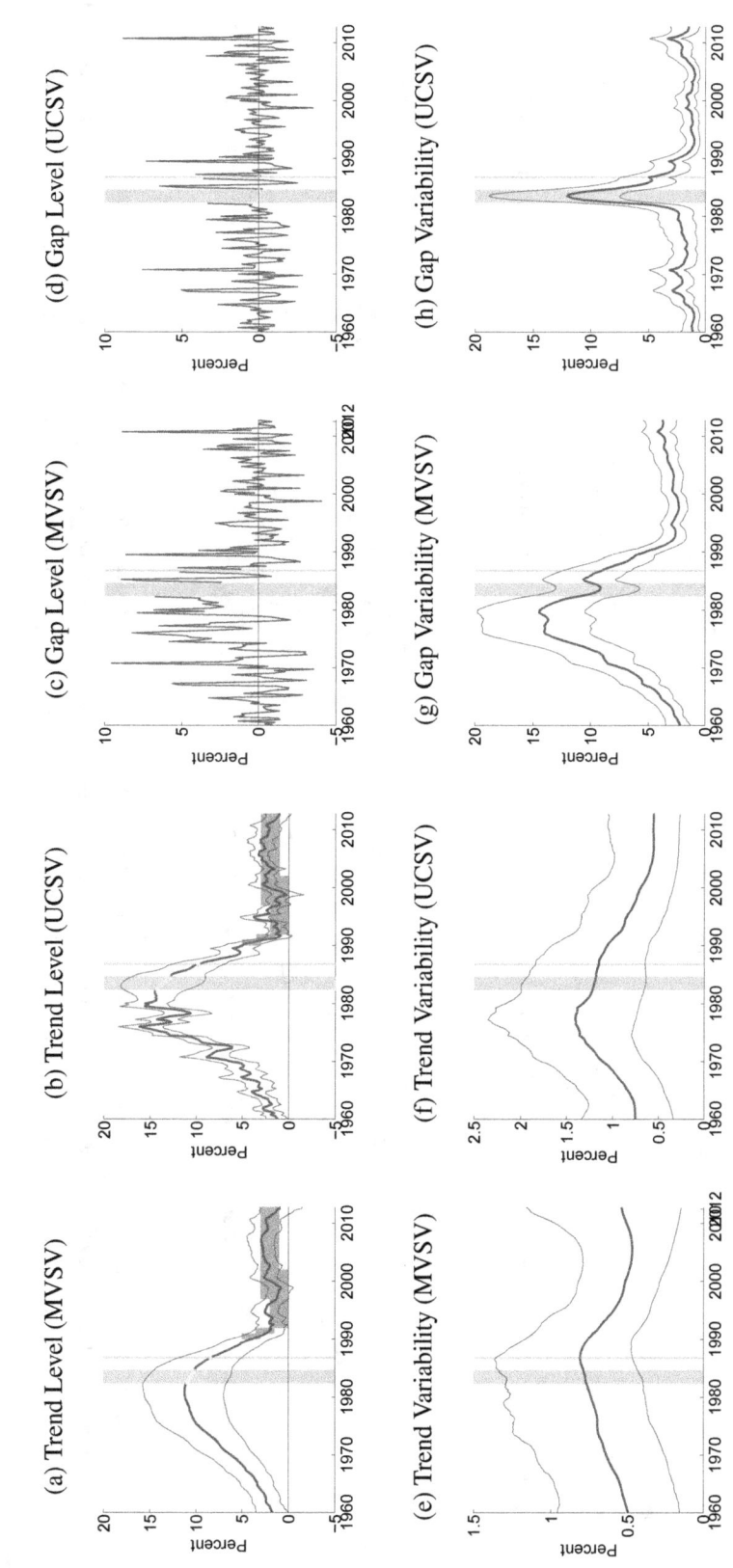

Note: Solid, thick blue lines show posterior means, and thinner blue lines depict 90% confidence sets derived from the model's posterior distribution conditional on all data. All levels are measured in annualized percentage points. Uncertainty is measured by the standard deviation of a quarterly trend shock. Data sources as listed in Table 1, using all available data since 1960. Grey shading marks dates in which data was excluded from computation due to shifts in the price index at that time. All country specific price shift dates for input measures are listed in Table 2. For those periods, estimated inflation gaps, shown in Panels (c) and (d), are marked green. When there are no price shift dates, the gap estimates are identical to the difference between actual inflation and the trend estimates, shown in Panels (a) and (b). In Panels (a) and (b), the solid red line marks the range of an offically stated inflation goal.

Figure 10: Spain

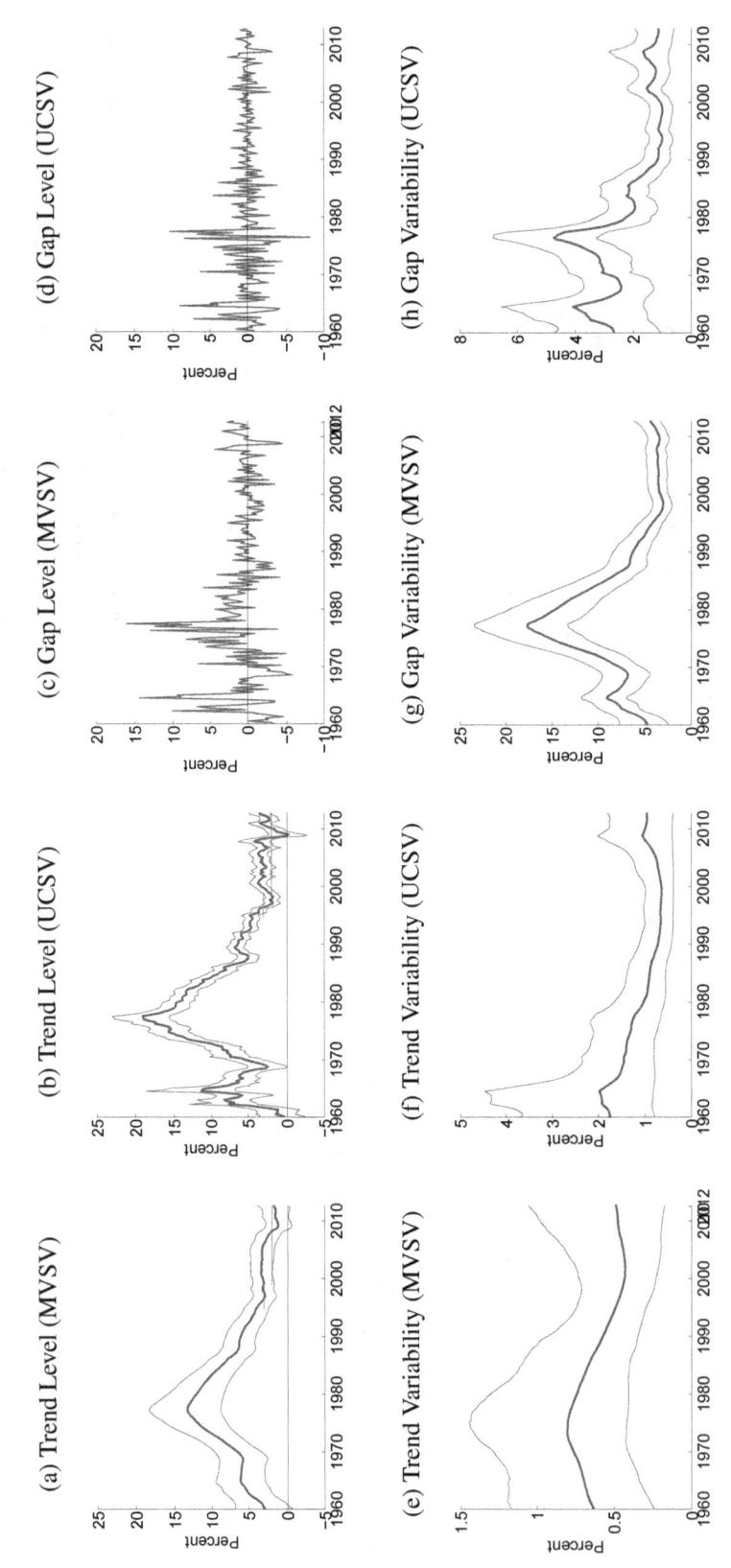

Note: Solid, thick blue lines show posterior means, and thinner blue lines depict 90% confidence sets derived from the model's posterior distribution conditional on all data. All levels are measured in annualized percentage points. Uncertainty is measured by the standard deviation of a quarterly trend shock. Data sources as listed in Table 1, using all available data since 1960. In Panels (a) and (b), the solid red line marks the level of an offically stated inflation goal.

Figure 11: Sweden

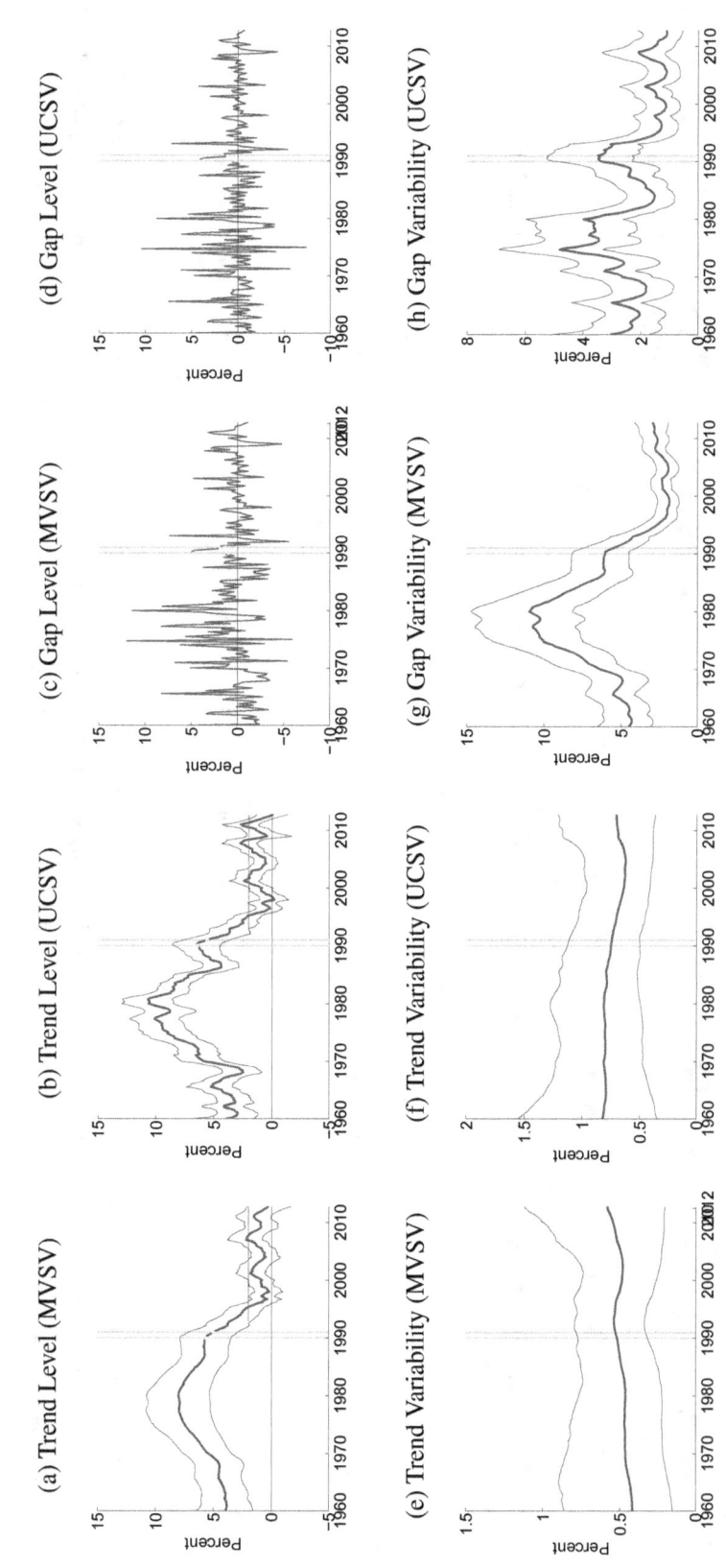

Note: Solid, thick blue lines show posterior means, and thinner blue lines depict 90% confidence sets derived from the model's posterior distribution conditional on all data. All levels are measured in annualized percentage points. Uncertainty is measured by the standard deviation of a quarterly trend shock. Data sources as listed in Table 1, using all available data since 1960. Grey shading marks dates in which data was excluded from computation due to shifts in the price index at that time. All country specific price shift dates for input measures are listed in Table 2. For those periods, estimated inflation gaps, shown in Panels (c) and (d), are marked green. When there are no price shift dates, the gap estimates are identical to the difference between actual inflation and the trend estimates, shown in Panels (a) and (b). In Panels (a) and (b), the solid red line marks the level of an officially stated inflation goal.

Figure 12: Switzerland

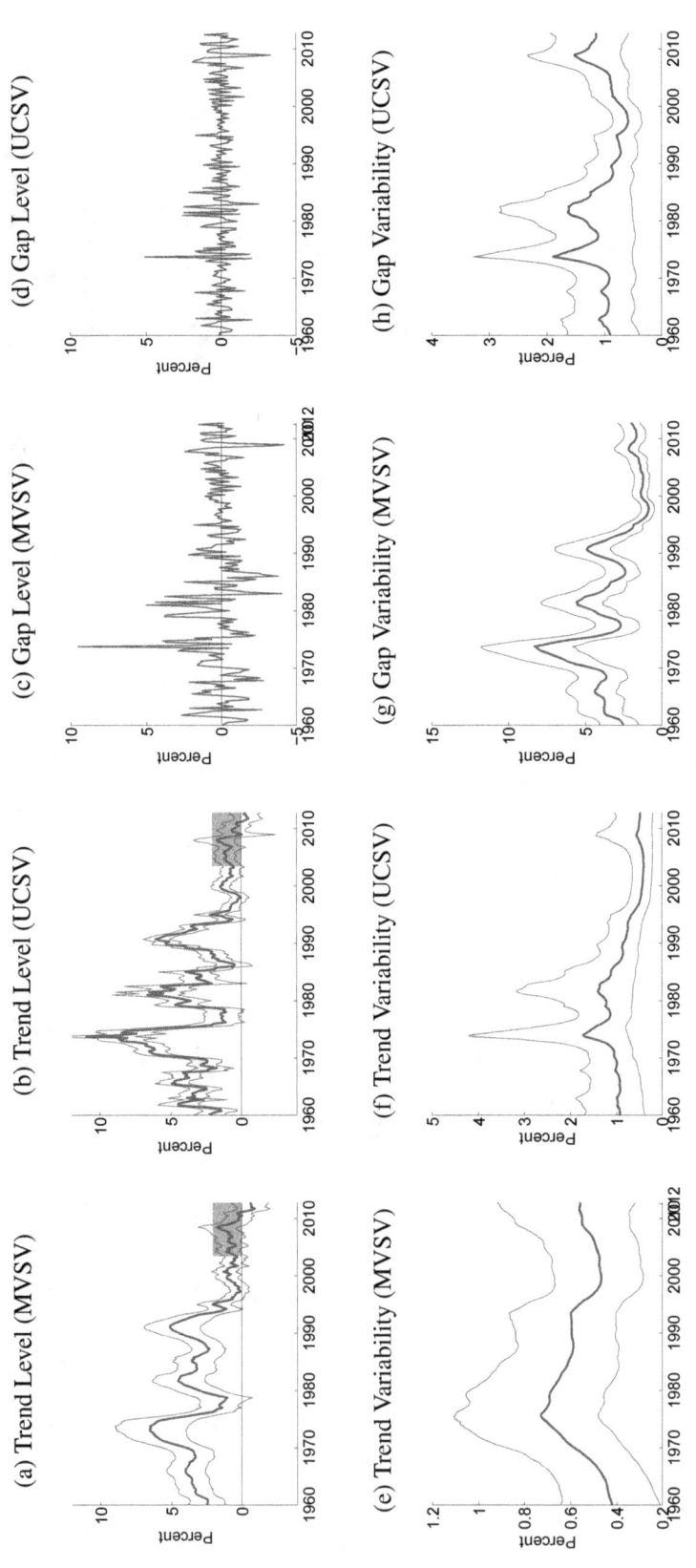

Note: Solid, thick blue lines show posterior means, and thinner blue lines depict 90% confidence sets derived from the model's posterior distribution conditional on all data. All levels are measured in annualized percentage points. Uncertainty is measured by the standard deviation of a quarterly trend shock. Data sources as listed in Table 1, using all available data since 1960. In Panels (a) and (b), the solid red line marks the range of an offically stated inflation goal.

Figure 13: United Kingdom

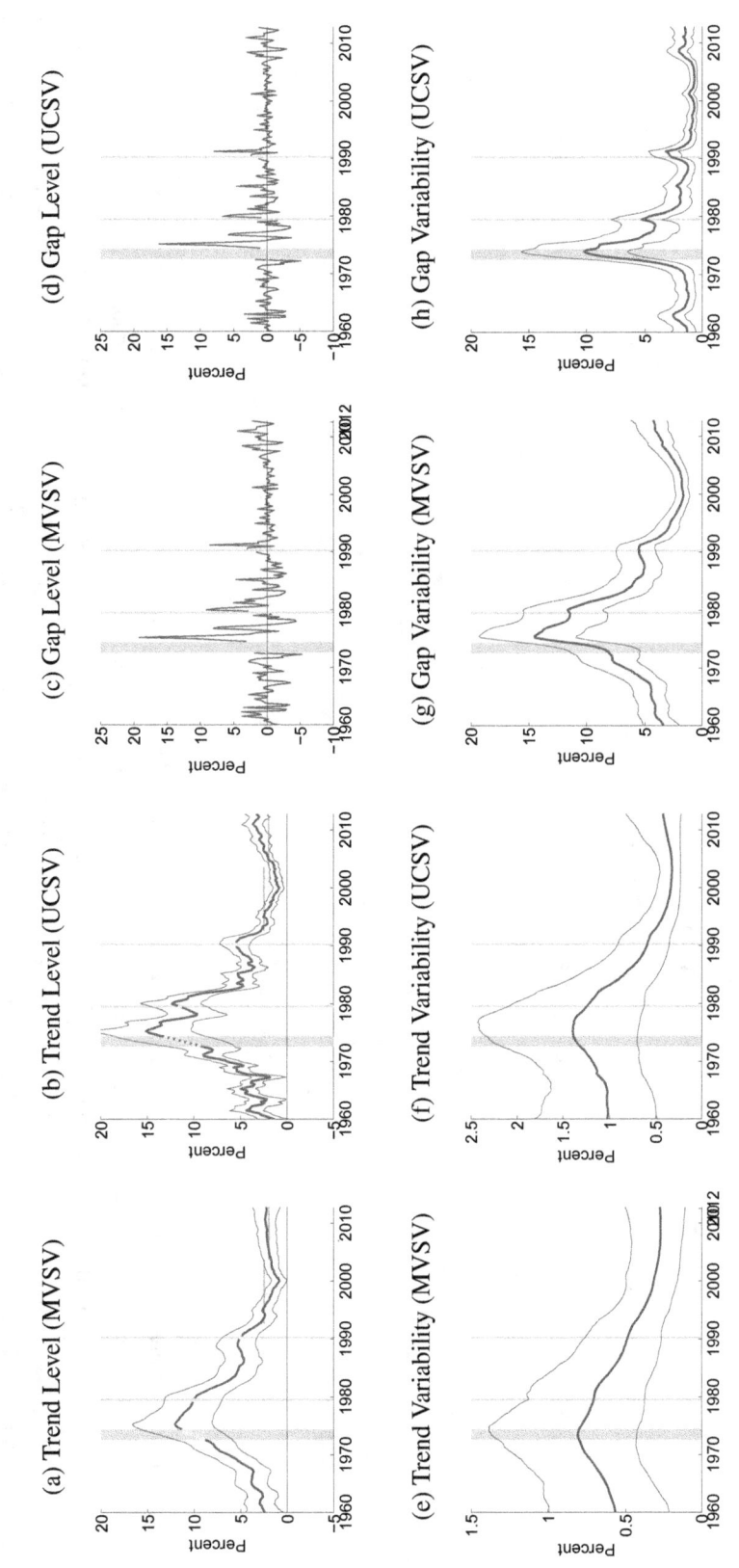

Note: Solid, thick blue lines show posterior means, and thinner blue lines depict 90% confidence sets derived from the model's posterior distribution conditional on all data. All levels are measured in annualized percentage points. Uncertainty is measured by the standard deviation of a quarterly trend shock. Data sources as listed in Table 1, using all available data since 1960. Grey shading marks dates in which data was excluded from computation due to shifts in the price index at that time. All country specific price shift dates for input measures are listed in Table 2. For those periods, estimated inflation gaps, shown in Panels (c) and (d), are marked green. When there are no price shift dates, the gap estimates are identical to the difference between actual inflation and the trend estimates, shown in Panels (a) and (b). In Panels (a) and (b), the solid red line marks the level of an offically stated inflation goal.

Figure 14: United States

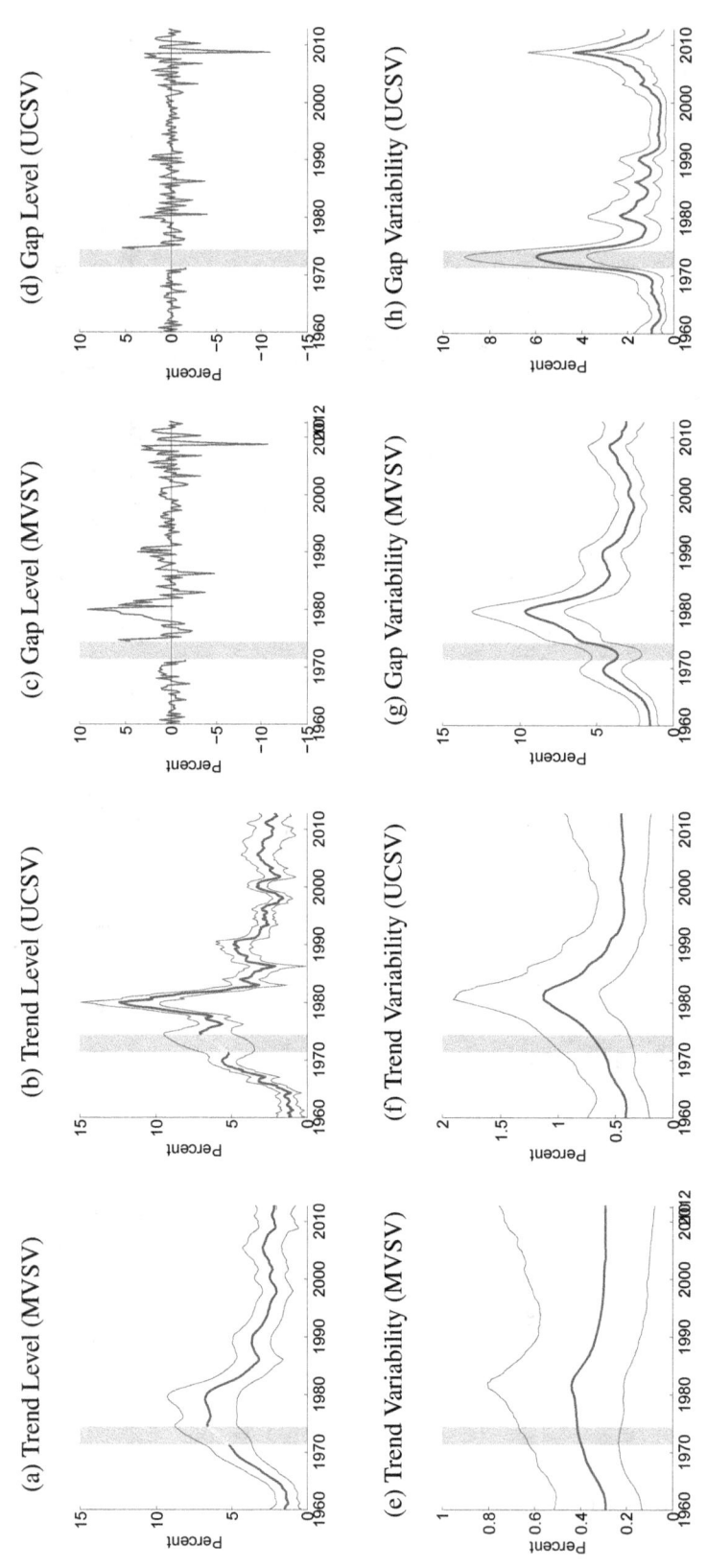

Note: Solid, thick blue lines show posterior means, and thinner blue lines depict 90% confidence sets derived from the model's posterior distribution conditional on all data. All levels are measured in annualized percentage points. Uncertainty is measured by the standard deviation of a quarterly trend shock. Data sources as listed in Table 1, using all available data since 1960. Grey shading marks dates in which data was excluded from computation due to shifts in the price index at that time. All country specific price shift dates for input measures are listed in Table 2. For those periods, estimated inflation gaps, shown in Panels (c) and (d), are marked green. When there are no price shift dates, the gap estimates are identical to the difference between actual inflation and the trend estimates, shown in Panels (a) and (b).

Figure 15: Trend Estimates and Price Shift Dates

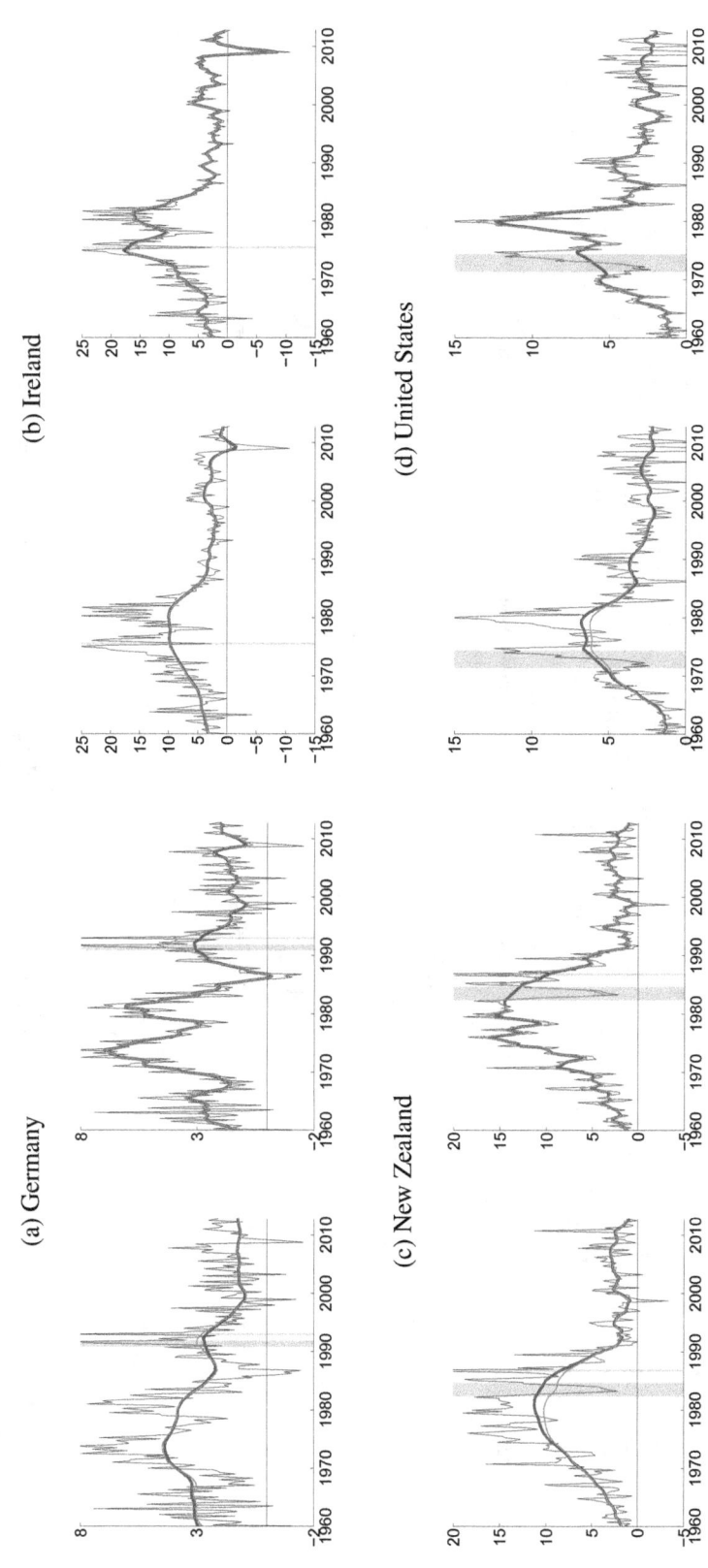

(a) Germany

(b) Ireland

(c) New Zealand

(d) United States

Note: In each panel, the left-hand side picture shows results from the MVSV model, the right-hand side picture has been generated from the UCSV model. Grey shading marks dates in which data was excluded from computation due to shifts in the price index at that time. All country specific price shift dates for input measures are listed in Table 2. Thin lines denote the actual data for inflation the headline CPI index. All levels are measured in annualized percentage points.

Figure 16a: Trend Estimates for MVSV Model

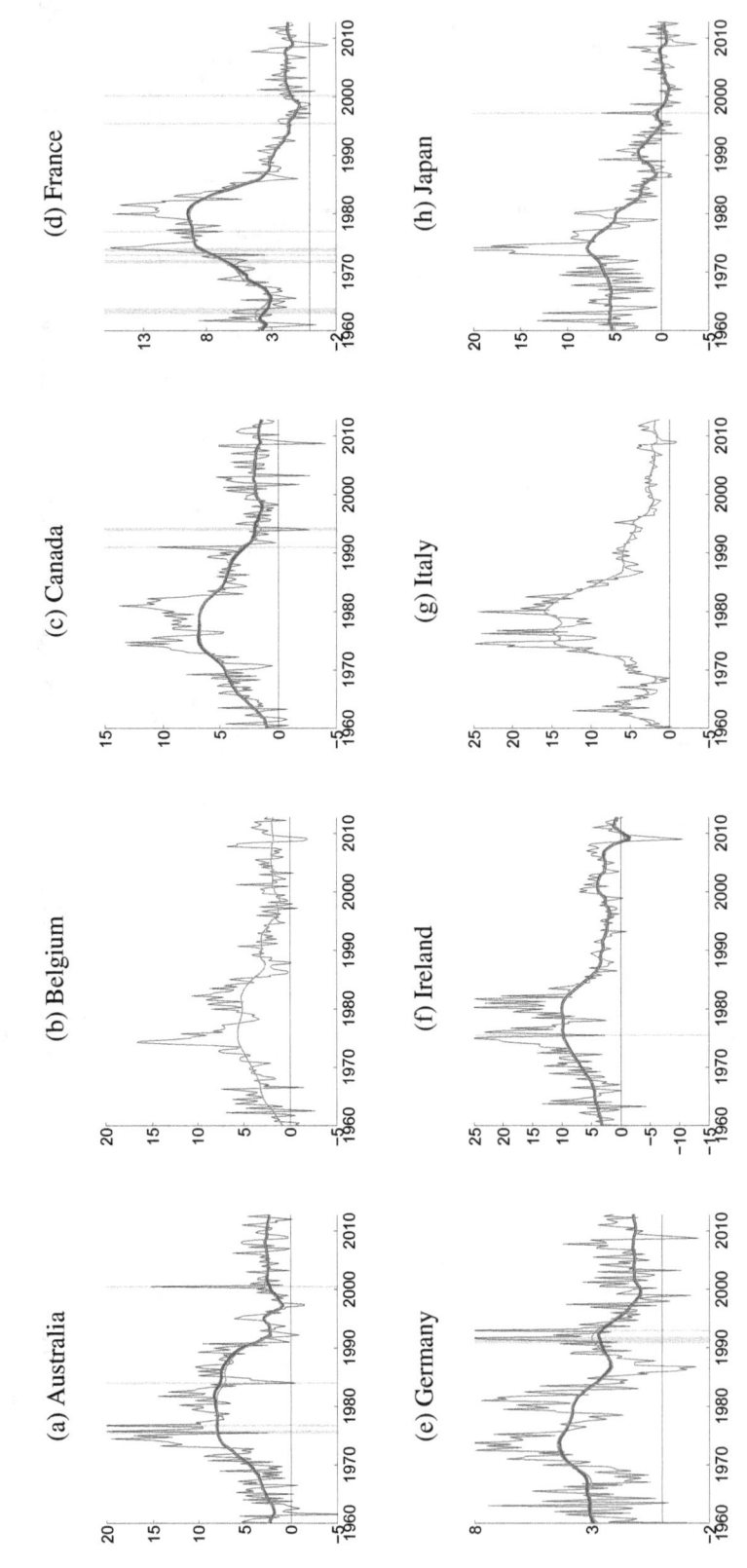

Note: Headline CPI inflation is shown in black, with the trend estimate including shift price dates in red. The trend estimate omitting price shift dates is shown in blue, with grey shading to indicate the specific time horizon (see Table 2).

Figure 16b: Trend Estimates for MVSV Model

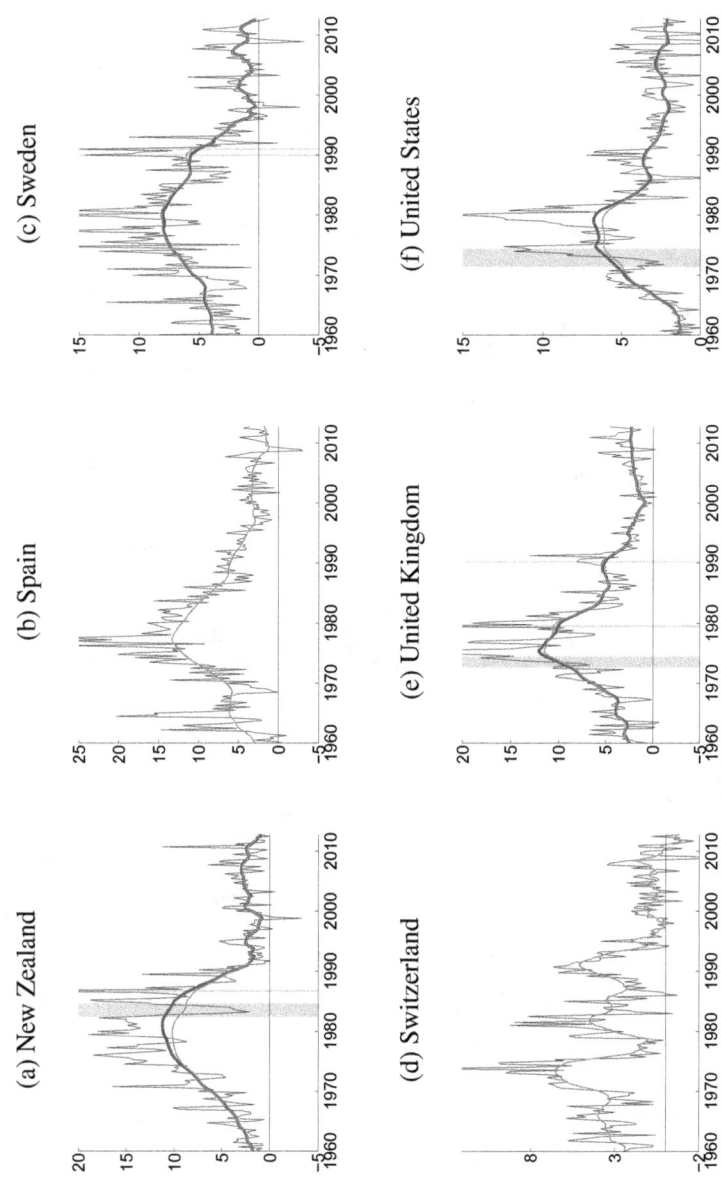

Note: Headline CPI inflation is shown in black, with the trend estimate including shift price dates in red. The trend estimate omitting price shift dates is shown in blue, with grey shading to indicate the specific time horizon (see Table 2).

Figure 17a: Trend Estimates for UCSV Model

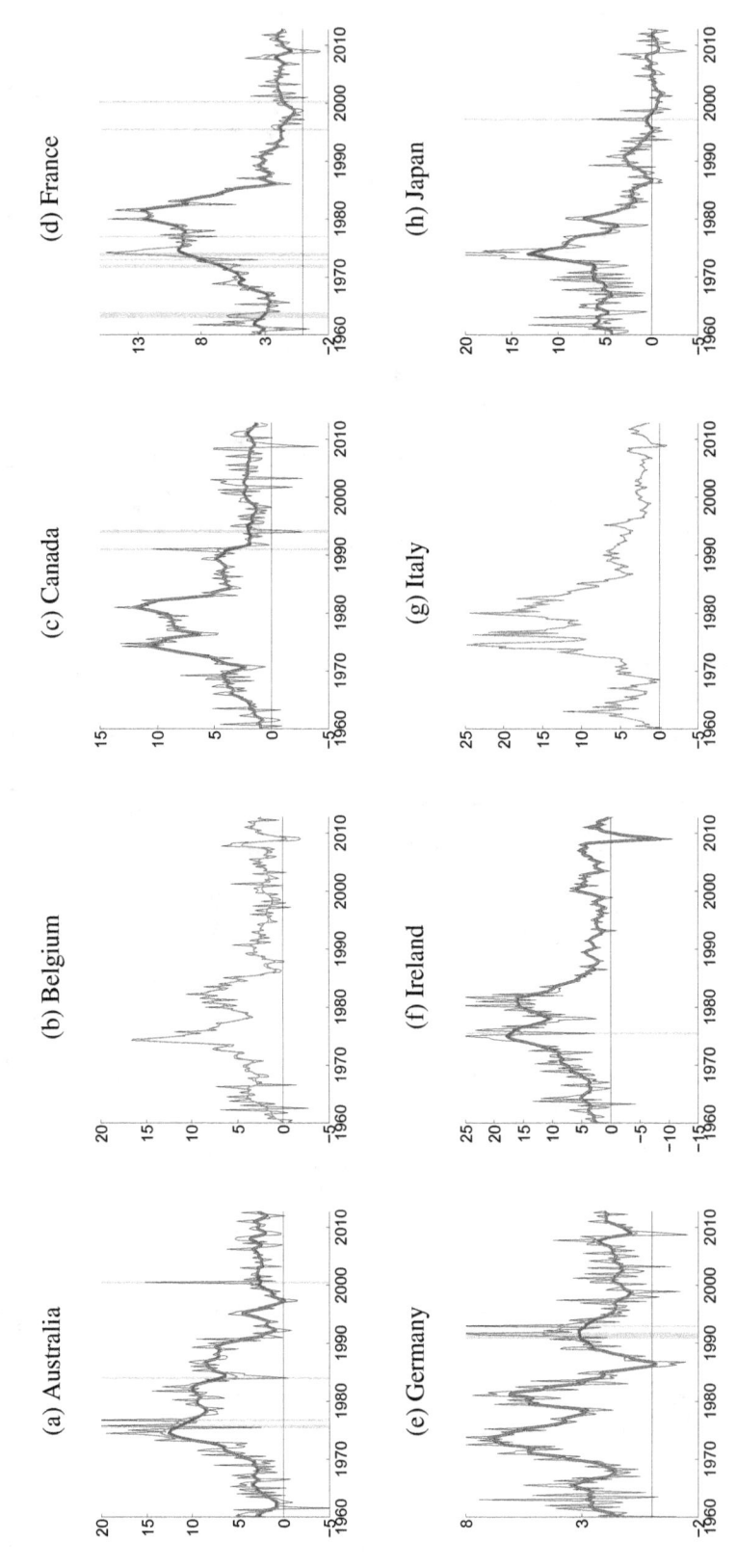

Note: Headline CPI inflation is shown in black, with the trend estimate including shift price dates in red. The trend estimate omitting price shift dates is shown in blue, with grey shading to indicate the specific time horizon (see Table 2).

Figure 17b: Trend Estimates for UCSV Model

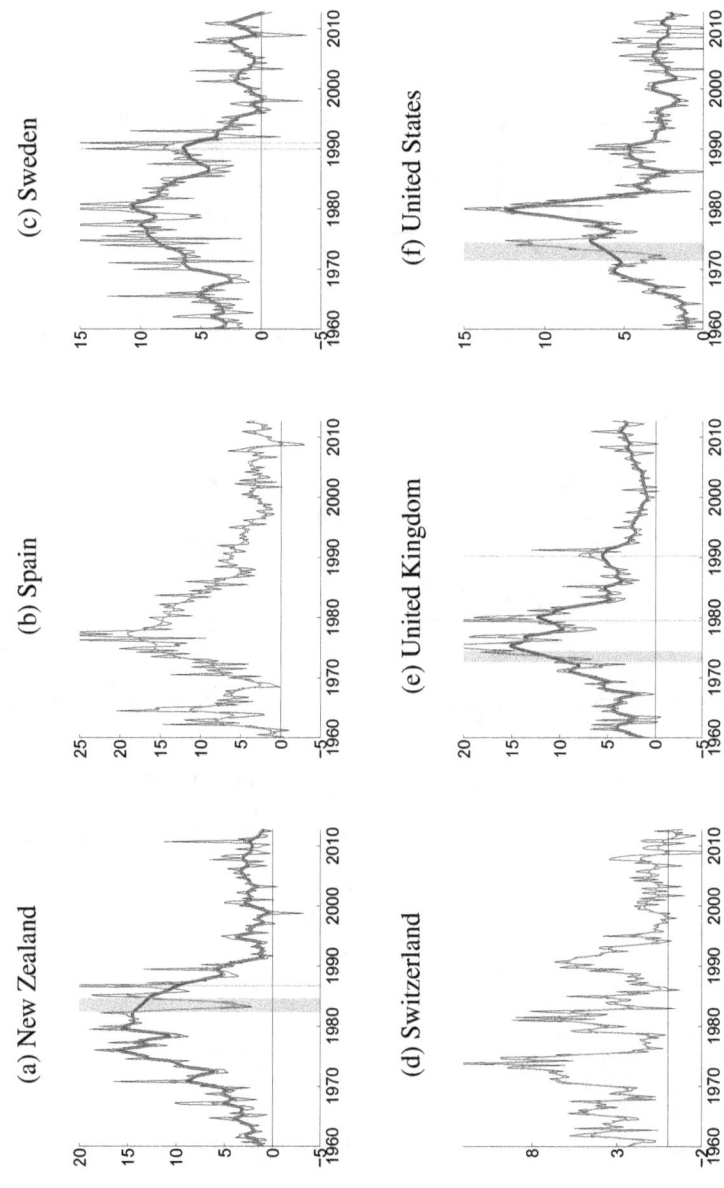

Note: Headline CPI inflation is shown in black, with the trend estimate including shift price dates in red. The trend estimate omitting price shift dates is shown in blue, with grey shading to indicate the specific time horizon (see Table 2).

Figure 18a: Filtered Trend Estimates

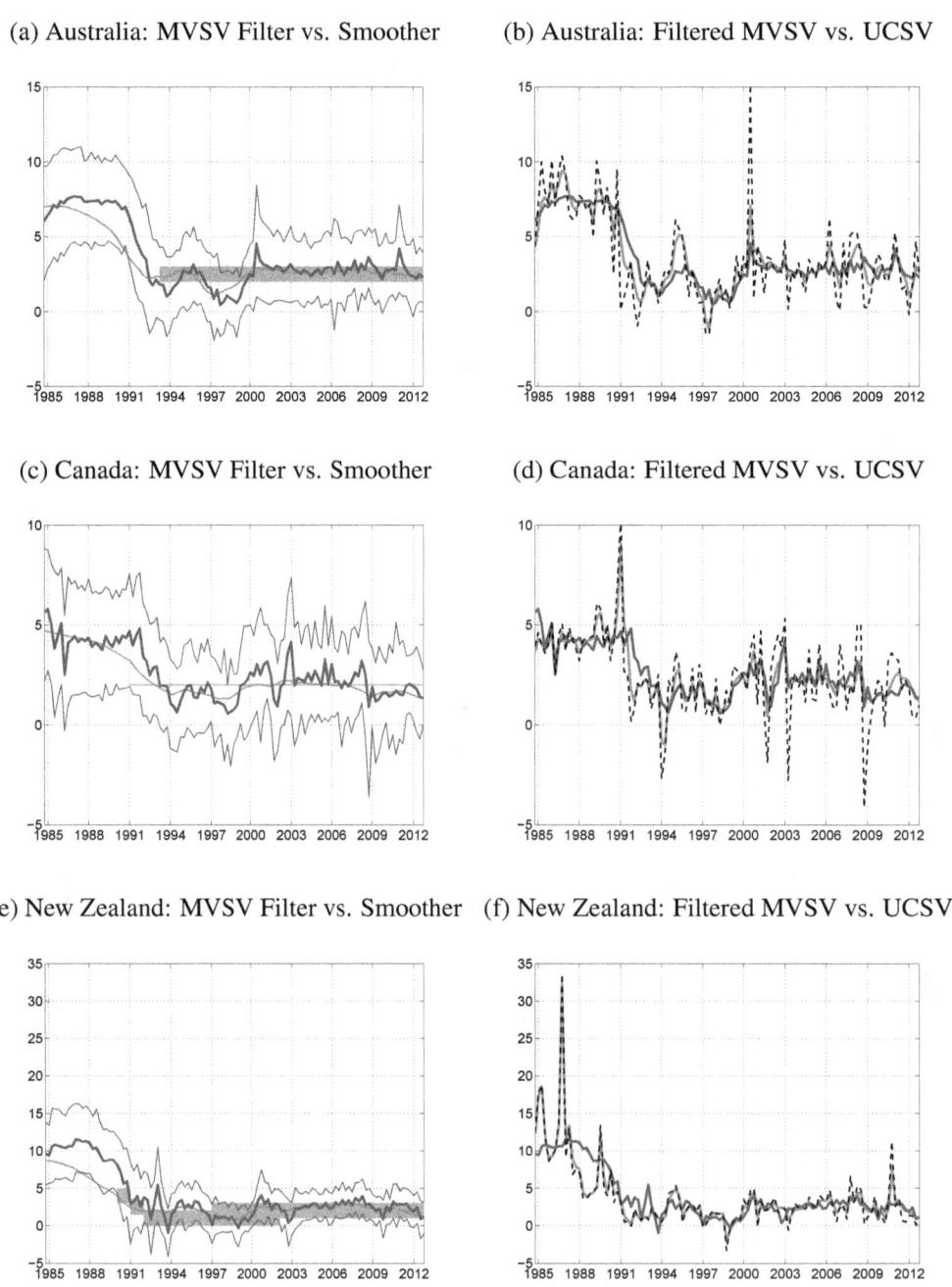

Note: Left-hand panels depict filtered trend estimates (solid blue line) from the MVSV model and their 90% confidence sets (thin blue lines) generated by pseudo-realtime forecasts using data from 1960:Q1 onwards. The solid red line depicts the corresponding smoothed trend estimates, which are conditioned on the entire data through 2012:Q4. Solid gray lines mark the range of an offically stated inflation goal. The right-hand side panels compare the filtered trend estimates of the MVSV model (solid blue line) against filtered estimates derived from the UCSV model (red line) as well as the actual data for headline CPI inflation (dashed black line).

Figure 18b: Filtered Trend Estimates (ctd.)

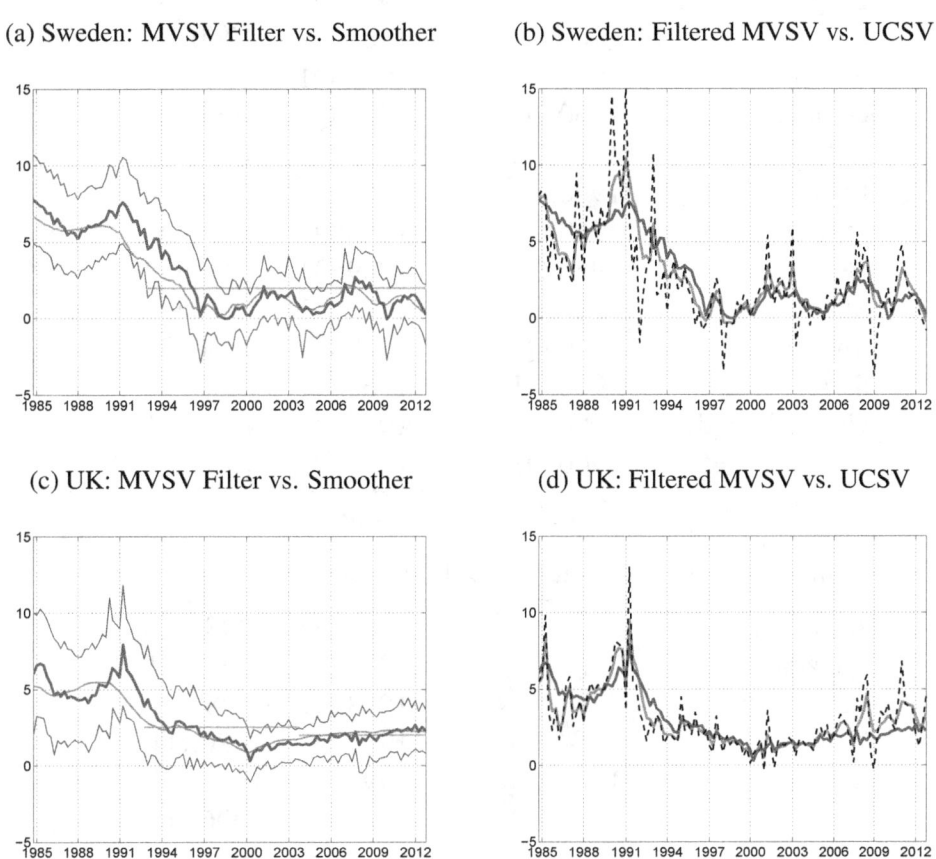

(a) Sweden: MVSV Filter vs. Smoother
(b) Sweden: Filtered MVSV vs. UCSV
(c) UK: MVSV Filter vs. Smoother
(d) UK: Filtered MVSV vs. UCSV

Note: Left-hand panels depict filtered trend estimates (solid blue line) from the MVSV model and their 90% confidence sets (thin blue lines) generated by pseudo-realtime forecasts using data from 1960:Q1 onwards. The solid red line depicts the corresponding smoothed trend estimates, which are conditioned on the entire data through 2012:Q4. Solid gray lines mark the range of an offically stated inflation goal. The right-hand side panels compare the filtered trend estimates of the MVSV model (solid blue line) against filtered estimates derived from the UCSV model (red line) as well as the actual data for headline CPI inflation (dashed black line).

Table 1: Data Overview

	Inflation Rates		
Country	Headline CPI	Core CPI	GDP Deflator
Australia	1960:Q1	1976:Q3	1960:Q1
Belgium	1960:Q1	1976:Q1	1980:Q1
Canada	1960:Q1	1961:Q1	1960:Q1
France	1960:Q1	1960:Q1	1960:Q1
Germany	1960:Q1	1962:Q1	1960:Q1
Ireland	1960:Q2	1976:Q1	1980:Q1
Italy	1960:Q1	1960:Q1	1960:Q1
Japan	1960:Q1	1970:Q1	1960:Q1
New Zealand	1960:Q1	1969:Q1	1981:Q2
Spain	1960:Q1	1976:Q1	1970:Q1
Sweden	1960:Q1	1970:Q1	1980:Q1
Switzerland	1960:Q1	1960:Q1	1970:Q1
United Kingdom	1960:Q1	1970:Q1	1960:Q1
United States	1960:Q1	1960:Q1	1960:Q1
	Inflation Goals		
Country	Inflation Goal	Dates	
Australia	2.0 – 3.0	1993:Q2 – EOS	
Canada	2.0	1991:Q1 – EOS	
Euro area[a]	2.0	1998:Q2 – EOS	
New Zealand	3.0 – 5.0	1990:Q1 – 1990:Q4	
	1.5 – 3.5	1991:Q1 – 1991:Q4	
	0.0 – 2.0	1992:Q1 – 1996:Q4	
	0.0 – 3.0	1997:Q1 – 2001:Q4	
	1.0 – 3.0	2002:Q1 – EOS	
Spain	3.0	1994:Q4 – 1998:Q4	
Sweden	2.0 ± 1	1993:Q1 – EOS	
Switzerland	<2.0	2003:Q3 – EOS	
United Kingdom	2.5	1992:Q4 – 2003:Q3	
	2.0	2003:Q4 – EOS	
United States	2.0	2012:Q1 – EOS	

Note: The model uses quarterly observations from 1960:Q1 through 2012:Q4. Countries with inflation goals continuing beyond the sample length are marked with EOS or end-of-sample. All variables are annualized and expressed in logs. Section 2 provides more information on the data sources.

[a] Belgium, France, Germany, Ireland, Italy, and Spain have all been Euro area countries since the currency area's inception.

Table 2: Omitted Price Shift Dates

Country	Date	Event
Australia	1975:Q3	Universal health insurance[a]
	1975:Q4	Sales tax increase[a]
	1976:Q4	Removal of universal health insurance[a]
	1984:Q1	Medicare introduction[a]
	2000:Q3	GST introduction[b]
Canada	1991:Q1	GST introduction[b]
	1994:Q1 – 1994:Q2	Cigarette tax change[b]
France	1963:Q1 – 1963:Q4	Controls on industrial prices[c]
	1971:Q4 – 1972:Q1	Price controls[c]
	1973:Q1	VAT decrease[c]
	1973:Q4 – 1974:Q1	Price controls[c]
	1977:Q1	VAT decrease[c]
	1995:Q3	VAT increase[c]
	2000:Q2	VAT decrease[c]
Germany	1991:Q1 – 1991:Q4	Reunification[b]
	1993:Q1	VAT increase[b]
Ireland	1975:Q3	Indirect tax cut[d]
Japan	1997:Q2	Consumption tax increase[b]
New Zealand	1982:Q3 – 1984:Q3	Price controls[d]
	1986:Q4	GST introduction[b]
Sweden	1990:Q1	VAT increase[b]
	1991:Q1	VAT increase[b]
United Kingdom	1972:Q4 – 1974:Q2	Price controls[a]
	1979:Q3	VAT tax increase[a]
	1990:Q2	Poll tax introduction[b]
United States	1971:Q3 – 1974:Q2	Nixon price controls[e]

[a] Neiss and Nelson (2005).
[b] Levin and Piger (2004, Table A2).
[c] Derived from OECD surveys and from our own analysis of news records.
[d] From our own analysis of news records.
[e] Frye and Gordon (1983).

Table 3: Forecast Evaluation: Annual Inflation Rates

		Years ahead				
		next	1 yr	2 yrs	3 yrs	4 yrs
Australia	*RMSE for MVSV*	1.75	2.28	2.50	2.62	2.74
	Relative to RW	0.85	0.83	0.84**	0.89***	0.93
	Relative to UCSV	0.97	0.95	0.92	0.91**	0.96
	Relative to MVSV-Trend	0.65***	0.78**	0.81**	0.82**	0.82***
Belgium	*RMSE for MVSV*	1.41	1.62	1.57	1.39	1.40
	Relative to RW	0.88	0.84	0.73	0.57	0.55
	Relative to UCSV	0.97	1.02	1.03	0.97	0.96
	Relative to MVSV-Trend	0.71***	0.83***	0.81***	0.79***	0.75***
Canada	*RMSE for MVSV*	1.43	1.40	1.53	1.66	1.75
	Relative to RW	1.00	0.88	0.70	0.64	0.62
	Relative to UCSV	0.97	0.95	0.87	0.90	0.89
	Relative to MVSV-Trend	0.70***	0.66***	0.71***	0.72***	0.74***
France	*RMSE for MVSV*	1.25	1.57	1.61	1.62	1.73
	Relative to RW	1.10	1.03	0.72	0.58	0.52
	Relative to UCSV	1.23	1.47	1.36	1.43	1.43
	Relative to MVSV-Trend	0.69**	0.92**	0.90***	0.89***	0.89***
Germany	*RMSE for MVSV*	1.18	1.49	1.48	1.57	1.67
	Relative to RW	1.01	0.94	0.78	0.71	0.66*
	Relative to UCSV	1.00	0.98	0.90	0.86	0.81*
	Relative to MVSV-Trend	0.66***	0.81***	0.80***	0.81***	0.83***
Ireland	*RMSE for MVSV*	2.04	2.53	2.52	2.45	2.41
	Relative to RW	0.81	0.78	0.61	0.53	0.46
	Relative to UCSV	0.91	0.82	0.80	0.90	0.96
	Relative to MVSV-Trend	0.71**	0.89	0.87	0.88	0.83**
Italy	*RMSE for MVSV*	1.47	2.08	2.04	2.01	2.10
	Relative to RW	1.15	1.02	0.73	0.57	0.50
	Relative to UCSV	1.28	1.31	1.21	1.23	1.29
	Relative to MVSV-Trend	0.72**	0.96*	0.95**	0.96	0.93***

Note: For each country, root-mean-squared errors (RMSE) are derived from out-of-sample forecasts that were generated from pseudo-realtime estimates of each model from 1985:Q1 onwards; each model estimation is conditioned on data from 1960:1 until the beginning of each forecast period. Superscripts *, **, and *** denote statistically significant differences in squared forecast errors—as computed from the test by Diebold and Mariano (1995)—at the 10%, 5%, and 1% level, respectively.

Table 3: Forecast Evaluation: Annual Inflation Rates (ctd.)

		Years ahead				
		next	1 yr	2 yrs	3 yrs	4 yrs
Japan	*RMSE for MVSV*	1.13	1.31	1.34	1.30	1.23
	Relative to RW	0.96	0.91*	0.83***	0.73**	0.60**
	Relative to UCSV	0.97	0.92	0.86***	0.82**	0.78**
	Relative to MVSV-Trend	0.66***	0.70***	0.73***	0.71***	0.74***
New Zealand	*RMSE for MVSV*	2.50	3.06	3.34	3.79	4.05
	Relative to RW	0.76	0.83	0.81	0.89	0.96
	Relative to UCSV	0.72	0.80	0.82	0.80	0.81
	Relative to MVSV-Trend	0.67**	0.75*	0.87**	0.90***	0.91**
Sweden	*RMSE for MVSV*	1.97	2.40	2.63	2.79	2.98
	Relative to RW	0.88	0.88	0.87	0.82	0.83
	Relative to UCSV	0.93	0.92	0.92	0.89	0.94
	Relative to MVSV-Trend	0.68***	0.78***	0.81***	0.83***	0.85**
Spain	*RMSE for MVSV*	1.48	1.89	1.98	1.94	2.10
	Relative to RW	0.92	0.99	0.84	0.70	0.67
	Relative to UCSV	1.02	1.10	1.08	1.05	1.14
	Relative to MVSV-Trend	0.70***	0.81***	0.85***	0.85***	0.83***
Switzerland	*RMSE for MVSV*	1.19	1.49	1.66	1.71	1.72
	Relative to RW	0.89*	0.91*	0.82*	0.72**	0.71
	Relative to UCSV	0.93	0.93	0.86*	0.77**	0.77*
	Relative to MVSV-Trend	0.72***	0.83***	0.87***	0.86***	0.89***
United Kingdom	*RMSE for MVSV*	1.32	1.66	1.87	1.92	1.98
	Relative to RW	0.97	0.98	0.91	0.74	0.57
	Relative to UCSV	0.96	0.99	0.93	0.87	0.90
	Relative to MVSV-Trend	0.68***	0.79***	0.84***	0.84***	0.84***
United States	*RMSE for MVSV*	1.36	1.35	1.34	1.41	1.28
	Relative to RW	0.87	0.84	0.77**	0.63**	0.45
	Relative to UCSV	0.92	0.91	0.82***	0.82**	0.77*
	Relative to MVSV-Trend	0.67*	0.69*	0.69*	0.67*	0.65*

Note: For each country, root-mean-squared errors (RMSE) are derived from out-of-sample forecasts that were generated from pseudo-realtime estimates of each model from 1985:Q1 onwards; each model estimation is conditioned on data from 1960:1 until the beginning of each forecast period. Superscripts *, **, and *** denote statistically significant differences in squared forecast errors—as computed from the test by Diebold and Mariano (1995)—at the 10%, 5%, and 1% level, respectively.

Table 4: Forecast Evaluation: Quarterly Inflation Rates

		Quarters ahead				
		1 qtr	4 qtrs	8 qtrs	12 qtrs	16 qtrs
Australia	*RMSE for MVSV*	2.28	2.68	2.92	3.07	3.20
	Relative to RW	0.94	0.94	0.90*	0.92**	0.96***
	Relative to UCSV	0.99	1.00	0.94	0.92*	0.94***
	Relative to MVSV-Trend	0.97*	1.00	1.00	1.00	1.00*
Belgium	*RMSE for MVSV*	1.70	2.00	1.95	1.93	1.77
	Relative to RW	0.98	0.94	0.84	0.77	0.63
	Relative to UCSV	1.07	0.97	1.01	1.02	0.93
	Relative to MVSV-Trend	0.94	1.02	1.00	1.00	1.00
Canada	*RMSE for MVSV*	2.01	2.06	2.12	2.16	2.30
	Relative to RW	0.99	1.02	0.97	0.82	0.77
	Relative to UCSV	1.04	0.95	0.96	0.88	0.96
	Relative to MVSV-Trend	1.07	1.02**	1.00	1.00	1.00
France	*RMSE for MVSV*	1.37	1.81	1.71	1.79	1.80
	Relative to RW	1.14	1.20	0.91	0.73	0.59
	Relative to UCSV	1.28	1.23	1.31	1.26	1.32
	Relative to MVSV-Trend	0.86*	1.00	1.00	1.00	1.00
Germany	*RMSE for MVSV*	1.52	1.76	1.84	1.86	1.95
	Relative to RW	1.04	1.04	0.93	0.83	0.76*
	Relative to UCSV	1.05	1.02	0.93	0.90	0.88
	Relative to MVSV-Trend	0.94	0.99	1.00	1.00	1.00
Ireland	*RMSE for MVSV*	2.16	2.84	2.86	2.91	2.78
	Relative to RW	0.94	0.87	0.79	0.66*	0.56
	Relative to UCSV	1.10*	0.90	0.82	0.84*	0.95
	Relative to MVSV-Trend	0.91**	1.00	1.00	1.00	1.00
Italy	*RMSE for MVSV*	1.55	2.06	2.17	2.15	2.08
	Relative to RW	1.30*	1.24	0.94	0.71	0.56
	Relative to UCSV	1.54**	1.27	1.24	1.16	1.22
	Relative to MVSV-Trend	0.93	1.00	1.00	1.00	1.00

Note: For each country, root-mean-squared errors (RMSE) are derived from out-of-sample forecasts that were generated from pseudo-realtime estimates of each model from 1985:Q1 onwards; each model estimation is conditioned on data from 1960:1 until the beginning of each forecast period. Superscripts *, **, and *** denote statistically significant differences in squared forecast errors—as computed from the test by Diebold and Mariano (1995)—at the 10%, 5%, and 1% level, respectively.

Table 4: Forecast Evaluation for Quarterly Inflation Forecasts (ctd.)

		Quarters ahead				
		1 qtr	4 qtrs	8 qtrs	12 qtrs	16 qtrs
Japan	*RMSE for MVSV*	1.65	1.73	1.86	1.84	1.82
	Relative to RW	0.99	0.97	0.94**	0.91**	0.82***
	Relative to UCSV	1.00	0.95	0.95	0.90***	0.87**
	Relative to MVSV-Trend	1.03	1.02*	1.00	1.00	1.00
New Zealand	*RMSE for MVSV*	3.42	3.74	4.11	3.85	4.20
	Relative to RW	0.91	0.86	0.91	0.76	0.88
	Relative to UCSV	0.89	0.80	0.85	0.84	0.84
	Relative to MVSV-Trend	0.99	1.00	1.00	1.00	1.00
Sweden	*RMSE for MVSV*	2.57	2.89	3.10	3.25	3.35
	Relative to RW	1.00	0.93	0.93	0.89	0.87
	Relative to UCSV	1.02	0.95	0.94	0.92	0.91
	Relative to MVSV-Trend	1.00	1.00	1.00	1.00	1.00
Spain	*RMSE for MVSV*	1.95	2.12	2.35	2.32	2.30
	Relative to RW	1.01	0.93	0.99	0.80	0.73
	Relative to UCSV	1.08	1.01	1.07	1.04	1.03
	Relative to MVSV-Trend	1.00	1.01	1.00	1.00	1.00
Switzerland	*RMSE for MVSV*	1.46	1.66	1.79	1.91	1.99
	Relative to RW	1.00	0.93	0.91	0.81*	0.75**
	Relative to UCSV	1.11*	0.92	0.93	0.84*	0.81**
	Relative to MVSV-Trend	0.97	1.00	1.00	1.00	1.00
United Kingdom	*RMSE for MVSV*	1.66	1.96	2.10	2.22	2.29
	Relative to RW	0.96	1.03	0.93	0.93	0.79
	Relative to UCSV	0.96	1.01	0.95	0.95	0.89
	Relative to MVSV-Trend	0.96*	1.01	1.00	1.00	1.00
United States	*RMSE for MVSV*	2.17	2.08	1.97	1.94	2.11
	Relative to RW	1.03	0.98	0.88	0.86**	0.76*
	Relative to UCSV	1.11	0.94	0.93	0.87**	0.90**
	Relative to MVSV-Trend	1.15	1.03	1.00	1.00	1.00

Note: For each country, root-mean-squared errors (RMSE) are derived from out-of-sample forecasts that were generated from pseudo-realtime estimates of each model from 1985:Q1 onwards; each model estimation is conditioned on data from 1960:1 until the beginning of each forecast period. Superscripts *, **, and *** denote statistically significant differences in squared forecast errors—as computed from the test by Diebold and Mariano (1995)—at the 10%, 5%, and 1% level, respectively.